MW01592168

Sick

A TRUE STORY

by Anna Gattone Kamide

DORRANCE
PUBLISHING CO
EST. 1920
PITTSBURGH, PENNSYLVANIA 15238

Dorrance Publishing Co
585 Alpha Drive
Pittsburgh, PA 15238
Visit our website at *www.dorrancebookstore.com*

ISBN: 978-1-6491-3236-9
eISBN: 978-1-6491-3719-7

I would like to dedicate this to my family, my friends, and the countless nurses and doctors who saved my life several times. I would like to thank everyone who contributed to this work. I appreciate all of your help. Thank you to the amazing judge who saved my ass big time by doing what is right and *allowing* her intelligence and emotion to interfere before I walked away with nothing. I am humbled by *ALL* of your generosity of heart, soul, and skills. To my readers, thank you for allowing me the honor of sharing my experiences with you.

This is a true story. It is a *study* in "the truth is stranger than fiction" adage… but true, nonetheless. Know that I write this, not to complain nor to draw sympathy. I tell this story as a cautionary tale to all. Be your own strong, well-informed medical advocate. Study your condition, ask questions, and do NOT be afraid to challenge the doctors.

It may be your only chance of survival once you are…

Sick

A True Story

The dream was *beyond* enchanting. I was ascending … *floating upwards* towards a beautiful bright light. Safely swaddled in a snuggly softness, never before had I felt such peace…just pure bliss. There was no pain, no fear, only benevolence.

My body was being guided lightly upwards by what felt to be loving hands and arms. I saw none, merely *felt* them. I could only *see* swirls of fluffy, cloud-like vapor. Above me, though, shining bright, was *that light*. I will never forget it! Such an intriguing bright light that I was intensely drawn to. It beckoned me, like the sight of a long lost loved one. I wanted *so* to be there. Watching the shadows dance off the fog-like smoke that surrounded me, I remember hearing classical music…I think it was Bach.

Mercifully unaware of what was *truly* unfolding around me, I continued on my mystical journey. I was rising. I was being pulled gently along, closer and closer to a large *palace* made entirely of what looked to be… *marshmallow fluff?* The light was coming from beyond that… *palace*, or whatever it was. I remember feeling a giddy excitement as if I were "going home"…finally going home after being away far too long.

I could almost interpret images imbedded in the soft white mist that surrounded me… surrounded everything. Trying to make sense of it, though, was difficult. I would see what looked to be a face, but then it would change. It was as if the images were…*fluid*…constantly shifting, similar to clouds on a windy day. I noticed the thick, billowy fog was coming together to form a tunnel. There were small, green random electric sparks flashing from it, like tiny bolts of lightning. I could feel my long hair floating statically towards the tunnel and upwards to the light. This undulating tunnel began to swirl closer around me, turning counterclockwise. Tightening as it rotated, it was as if it were attempting to hug me. Beyond it, that *light* drew me in magnetically. It was so bright yet not at all hard on the eyes. With my arms stretched out, I *swam* through the air to reach the light. Somehow, I knew that if I could just get to it, I would…*everything* would…be alright. I can *still* remember that enchanted feeling, so free and filled with joy. I moved my head slightly to take in my surroundings, smiling as the softness soothed me. Looking up, I stared in awe of the inviting light. Desperately, I needed to know more *about* this palace and this light. I needed to *get* there! I was SO close, almost to the point of *reaching* it when I was jarred awake by intense, *indescribable* **PAIN.**

What the…?

I opened my heavy eyes and turned my head slightly, causing even **MORE** pain…*new* pain.

What exactly is hurting me? Is it… Everything?! *Oh, God, yes!*

Everything *hurts and it hurts really bad. Why?*

I searched my mind to remember where I was and what was happening to me. I felt frozen…paralyzed. It was as if I were trapped inside myself, unable to do anything except see, albeit poorly… and feel intense pain.

My body lay in the supine position on an icy steel gurney. Shifting my eyes downward towards my chest, I saw two blood stained tubes protruding from that area. Instantly I thought about PVC piping for pools. I realized that the majority of my pain was coming from…*whatever* these are.

Had I fallen into a dumpster filled with PVC?!

I was cold, freezing cold. The sharp smell of rubbing alcohol was prominent in the air. The lighting was harsh… *brutal* actually. I thought of the soothing light of my dream and of how completely opposite the types of light were. My thoughts were cut short by an incredible rush of agony.

Geez!

This pain…. my *GOD*, the pain…it felt as though I was on FIRE. Desperately, I searched my mind for an explanation. Attempting to push past the intense, stabbing excruciation, I tried to look around to take in my surroundings. I was only able to move my head slightly without sending waves of torment through my body. Panicking, I searched my mind fervently…

Think! I chided myself. *THINK! Think thinkthinkthinkthink*

WHAM!

There was a sudden, ridiculously loud noise exactly next to my left ear. I didn't so much *hear* it as I did *feel* it. Jolts of intense pain coursed through my entire body as I had instinctively jerked away. My eyes caught a quick glimpse of a stainless-steel wastepaper basket that, oddly enough, was right next to my head. It was still slightly moving from its encounter with…*whatever* was thrown into it. Just as I realized that the "sound from hell" came from this innocuous item, I noticed a human form standing directly over me. Aghast at the pain that was ripping through my entire body, I tried to concentrate on the sight in front of my eyes.

It's a person!

OH, THANK GOD! Help me please!

A female figure loomed over me. She was all in white with her hands on her ample hips, head tilted to one side.

Help me please! Oh, my God, please help me!

I was shocked when I realized that she wasn't even flinching as I begged. I then became aware that the words weren't even coming out of my mouth!

*I can't **TALK**!?*

The pain throughout my body was so horrific that I was unable to lift my head closer to her to try to whisper, so I squinted…in an effort to see her face. My scope of vision was surrounded by a haze of light that became blurrier as it faded away at the edges. I attempted to convey my need through my eyes…pleading with whomever it was. I remember trying to adjust my vision to the harsh lighting so that I could see her more clearly…

Wait, is she… smiling?

Oh *yeah*, she was. She was grinning down at me sardonically…*evil* even.

"Two points!" a different voice from behind me jubilantly exclaimed. I could hear two women laughing. As my mind began to clear, I realized that the horrible sound came from a second woman, behind me, throwing something very heavy into that stainless-steel wastepaper basket that was curiously positioned right next to my head. At first this made no sense to me. It would become only *too* clear soon.

I desperately attempted to look around the room, trying to put words to what I was seeing…

But the PAIN!

Is that why I am so confused?

I took an extremely good look at the…

Nurse…nurse?…That's a nurse!

Okay, so I'm in the hospital.

My initial reaction to the realization of knowing my whereabouts was relief. I was safe and in a hospital. The comfort, however, was short-lived, rapidly changing to horror as the towering nurse above me began to emit a laugh. It was an *evil* laugh, and it sent chills down my aching spine. On the verge of panic, I desperately tried to make sense of the ridiculous situation I found myself in.

Okay…so I'm in the hospital and the nurses are…

Torturing me?! Wait…*what?*

I literally shook my head as if to physically lose the thought, and the agony that it caused is difficult to describe. I can remember thinking…

I'm on fire…I must be…I feel like *I'm on fire!*

The room was alive with hostility. The conglomeration of evil malice from the nurses combined with my pain and misery made for an indescribably anxiety-ridden atmosphere. Then there was the beeping… *so much beeping!* Incessant, persistent, and competitive beeping! I listened as several separate rhythmic sounds created a cacophony of high-pitched mechanical screaming. The noise echoed throughout my pounding head. I longed for my dream to continue, the painless peace I felt only minutes ago cruelly belied this world of pain. Straining against the agony, I could see that there were others in the room, lying down across from me…plastic tubes snaking from their bodies. Evil nurse number one was now a mere inch from my ear. I wanted to pull away from her but could *not* due to the unrelenting pain. The smell from her wrinkled smock was of sour sweat and cigarette smoke. When she opened her mouth to speak, I nearly gagged on the odor of onion. In a sinister whisper, I heard…and *felt* her say, "Whatsamatter, ***junkie?*** Not having fun yet?" Her tone was harsh, cold, and dripping with disdain. Desperately, I searched my mind for an explanation.

A dream…that's it…I'm just having a nightmare…

*Junkie? What is a junkie again? Why can't I **think**?*

Electric jolts of pain surged through my neck as I moved my head, a sudden realization causing extreme panic…

Hold on…There is no PAIN in dreams! This is actually happening!

Ah, shit.

Salty tears streamed down my face and into my mouth. The snot from my nose settling on the thick of my dry upper lip.

I attempted to study my surroundings.

…so blurry…

My eyes, desperately trying to make sense of what was right in front of them, caught the direct stare of another set gazing right back at me from a bed across the room…

Oh YES!…I will ask HER!

Opening my mouth to speak felt wrong. My jaw was too heavy, my lips far too dry. Desperate to communicate, however, I pushed the air out of my mouth with as much force as I was able. The sound in my head did *not* match what I heard,

ARGSQUEEK! UGH-ARGASQUEEKEEK!

What …?

I could not speak! I was mortified when, in place of words, this breathy, shrill sound had come out of me.

Is that my VOICE?

It was raspy and fractured, squeaking not unlike that of a broken windshield wiper in a spotty rain. My thoughts raced. The pain coursed through my body like an EMP pulse. Out of nowhere, for whatever reason, my mind began to display images. Memories…as if it mercifully wanted to comfort me with snapshots in my head of better times. I saw my husband laughing, my children playing, there were holidays and vacation images. I saw pets that had passed away, clips of friends and family get-togethers. I wondered if this was my "life flashing in front of me" before death. I distinctly remember thinking,

*Oh, just **take** me, for fuck's sake; this is unbearable.*

My thoughts were interrupted by the frightening sight of "evil nurse number one" in my face again. I *smelled* her before my eyes focused properly on her. She was leaning in so close that, fearfully, I closed my eyes as she spoke.

"I'm sorry…what's that *junkie*?" she asked loudly, her tone was condescending and disingenuous for all to hear. Leaning in closer, she dramatically feigned hearing a response. I was horrified.

This is so way messed UP!

The woman across the room in her hospital bed whose eyes had met mine was now conveying pity to me. She looked at me, then looked at the nurses, and quickly looked away, frightened. Just as I was about to attempt eye contact with another roomie, evil nurse number two blocked my view. Animated…as if performing, her eyes large, hands up to her mouth, she projected her voice to the entire room, "My GOODNESS, NO! There are no drug dealers here." Her voice was shrill and her Ss were hissed. My mind raced.

*OK…What am I missing here!? What the fuck is a junkie again…? Why can I not think? Junkie..? Junkie! Wait…I **do** know what a junkie is! Oh, shit. Hold on, I'm not a junkie! Why is this happening?*

"Now, Anna" she announced loudly, "these drugs are for *sick* people!"

Then she leaned in closely and spit in my face as she called me a bitch. I probably should have tried to ingest it, as it would be the only liquid I would receive for hours. Six hours and some change to be exact.

There I was, fresh out of a very sketchy open-heart surgery, left to suffer without *any* pain medicine, fluids, or humane care by two sadistic, judgmental pieces of shit "nurses."

Maybe it was the anger from being thought of as a junkie and called a bitch, or the images that kept popping into my mind, I don't know, but suddenly, a rush of memories swept through me…a montage of the last three months played in my head like an old movie, and although it was fractured and not perfectly clear, I became aware of the nightmare I was currently in. Suddenly I *knew* what was going on…I knew **everything**.

OHSWEETBABYJESUS!

Tears streamed down my face as my memory came flooding back. After putting it all together, I *knew* why I was here. I had come to the hospital for open heart surgery to repair the valve that was so hideously destroyed by the infection I acquired from a severely botched hysterectomy! This incredible pain must be *normal* for post open heart. Wow. There were just a few things I couldn't figure out. Why wouldn't I have been given pain medicine?

... why am I being tormented?! Why would she call me a JUNKIE? *I'm not a junkie!*

It would all be explained to me later, once I woke to a host of suits standing around my hospital bed after the *second* heart surgery which was necessary after I fell from the gurney during my torment. I had coded (died) and needed to be reopened which caused my sternum to splinter and my ribs to shatter. This necessitated a manual cardiac massage. I was dead for many minutes before Dr. Bakhos, with my heart in his hands, literally, massaged it and brought me back to life. Unbeknownst to me, the infection that I acquired from the horrific hysterectomy was often seen in IV drug users. I was riddled with needle marks from needing to be in the hospital for weeks prior to the surgery as my heart kept failing. Back in 1999, they drew blood every eight hours, and the IVs were not equipped to draw from the catheter used as your intake IV. I *looked* like an intravenous drug user. Not bothering to learn my *actual* history, the evil nurses from hell just assumed that I was a drug addict. A *junkie*. As if it were okay to torture me then. They also saw that the waiting room was filled to capacity with my loved ones waiting to see how surgery went, and they were pissed off that I had so many friends and family there supporting me. Me...the *junkie*. Those heartless bitches tortured me for a little over six hours. They tied my long hair in knots and cut it in random places, they deliberately slammed into the gurney I was on, causing me intense pain. They positioned a small steel garbage can next to my head and played bozo buckets using glass trash. The worst, however, is that my sternum had just been *sawed open* and they ignored the order to give me pain medicine. They laughed as I thrashed my body screaming in pain. There is no way to properly describe the horror I experienced. I only wanted to die. I begged pathetically for the cruel nurses...some-one...*anyone* to help me. Help me or *kill* me.

I had never known such evil. I felt so helpless. I begged God to take me. Take me back to the tunnel of fluff, to that light! I writhed and cried pathetically trying so hard to make the pain better until I finally fell off of the gurney.

I landed on my left side and the chest tube located there was shoved violently into my body, piercing my left lung. Surprisingly, I screamed...I didn't think I even *could*. The evil tag team clumsily tossed me back on the slab of steel. They both found it funny...

A real belly laugh for both of them! ...until my heart stopped beating.

It was then that something amazing occurred.

The first thing I noticed was the smell. A beautiful scent of lilies and some other amazing floral scent. I looked up through my tears and saw the face of an angel. She was a nurse unlike the others...her uniform was from an earlier era, 1950s at least, and she wore an old-fashioned nurse's hat pinned to her beehive hairdo. An inner light emanated *from* her... making her face luminous, and I could *feel* her kindness as she softly touched my arm. We looked deeply into each other's eyes. I felt as if we were communicating telepathically...*somehow*. She resembled my Sister Martha and just *looking* at her brought me comfort...relief. Strangely I knew to be as quiet as possible, and that I was being rescued. My heart leapt with hope as my angel nurse deftly disconnected the many medical attachments that were like chains of steel to me. I could feel the movement of the gurney I was on and knew we were leaving that horrid room. I couldn't turn my head enough to look back at my rescuer, but I *knew* she was there. Suddenly, I felt an intense head rush and then the magical feeling of *pain relief* swept through me. Thankfully, I embraced the feeling and sunk deep into myself.

OhthankyouGod

Mercifully, it was as if someone was closing the curtains, and I was the stage. Black began on either side of my vision and slowly came together like the curtains of an all-encompassing theater until I passed out.

Basically, my Dear Reader... on my thirty-fifth birthday, I underwent what I was *told* was an emergency partial hysterectomy. It was so poorly done and so unethically followed up on that it ruined the rest of my life thus far. Repercussions and complications fell like dominos...oh, who am I kidding? They're *still* falling.

I wish I had a dollar...no, a *medical solution* for every time someone has said to me

"You should write a book!"

So, I did. The details are horrifying and sound like a bad movie plot, but this is truly how it went down. Oh, and it only took me twenty years to write this! Seriously, thanks for reading, I sincerely hope you enjoy it. More so, I hope that it somehow helps someone… somewhere.

It was May of 1999. The weather was finally tolerable following an inordinately severe winter. The world worried irrationally about the upcoming shift into a new millennium. It was amazing how many people actually thought that the world was going to come to an end. This was the least of my concerns, and ironically enough, *my* world truly WAS coming to an end…I just didn't know it yet….

I was clueless.

My worst problem at the time was my monthly period. I was getting cramps galore and bleeding for three out of four weeks. I spent my busy days trying to deal with the cramps and the heavy flow, forging ahead with my relentless schedule.

In retrospect, I was micro-managing too much at one time; I had tediously planned a huge birthday bash for my two boys, was planning an exciting road trip adventure with my best friends and *dreading* an upcoming surgery. Not exactly in that order. Had I known that my life was about to be turned upside down and STAY that way for twenty years, perhaps I would have… *somehow*… prepared for it or even protected myself from it. What an incredibly *sick* feeling, knowing that one poorly made decision began the domino effect of medical mishaps that created the nightmare I am currently trying to survive. Actually, calling my current medical condition a nightmare is quite generous… more accurately, since 1999, it has been a living HELL on Earth. I suppose I could say that I'm just having a *really* bad millennium.

The '90s were *amazing* but went by too quickly. In 1999 I was on top of my game though; I had the world by its short and curlies, and I was loving every hectic minute of it. I answered to no one and made the rules up as I went along. I was running my business, raising my boys, selling real estate on the side, riding horses as much as possible, and playing on at least one softball team a season, not to mention being committed to every one of the four *billion* extracurricular activities my two boys were involved in, and oh yes, their schools. If I wasn't checking for head lice or mentoring, I was substitute teaching or handing out free lunches.

Life was non-stop until you drop. When I needed to let some steam out, I would drive an hour away to where I would help a friend out who owned a dude ranch. He let me ride as much as I wanted, which ever horse I wanted, and I would lead customers out on guided horse trail rides. He made the money they paid; I got to keep my tips. Life was hectic, and even a bit danger-ous at times, but I felt like I had achieved my dream.

I was a no-nonsense, work hard/play hard ageless American Dream Queen. I drove a brand-new Mercedes…the funny thing is that I am *still* driv-ing it due to the massive reversal of fortune. Yes, it is almost twenty years old, go ahead, laugh about it…I do! I just love her though! The old girl has still *got it* too…I'm talking about the car, not me. I, on the other hand, am now a fuck-ing monster. Yes, my Dear Reader, life kicked my ass *but good*, as you will see if you choose to read on… I am now horribly disfigured … but we will get to that. Now, where was I? Ah yes, so I had been experiencing incredible cramp-ing, and I had my monthly for the whole damn month so….

Upon the advice of a trusted friend, Linda Engler, I saw a popular ob-gyn surgeon. Linda is a great lady, and this doctor had diagnosed her cancer and saved her life. I had heard of the same doctor through other women as well, so I decided to make an appointment. After a consult and an examination, she immediately ordered a laparoscopy for two days later.

Following the exploratory laparoscopy, the doctor told me I needed an emergency hysterectomy to correct a very dangerous uterine condition. I was warned that to put this surgery off could cause my uterus to rupture, which the doctor thought to be full of infection, thus bringing peritonitis to all my organs, possibly causing my death. Surgery would need to be done and done soon. Feeling as though I had no choice, I was off to hysterectomyland. Mean-while, unbeknownst to me, my doctor had chosen her lover… the fellow doctor with whom she was carrying on an illicit extra-marital affair, to be her assistant surgeon for my hysterectomy. This, in and of itself was wrong, the trial proving later that the additional assistance of another doctor wasn't even required. It was just two doctors trying to make each other more money… professional networking using the human bodies of others I suppose.

Now, these two doctors, who were both married, mind you…just not to *each other*, and according to later deposition testimony by the attending nurses, were flirting and bickering throughout the entire surgery. What *should* have been a forty-five-minute common medical procedure turned into an hour-long *bad* Sonny and Cher impression and a three-hour desperate search for the fallopian tube that she *dropped* into my body and was unable to retrieve. Instead of owning up to the fact that a mistake had been made, *my* doctors chose to cover it up. They put an unknown piece of tissue into a jar of formalin and sent it off to pathology labeled "right fallopian tube." To add insult to injury, the dynamic duo scraped and searched for my *real* tube in vain, doing even *more* damage to my internal organs and creating a shocking amount of scar tissue and future illnesses from organ trauma.

Following the hysterectomy, I was in severe pain for weeks. Upon my follow-up visit, the doctor examined me. She tells me that it is a *mystery* to her why I would still be in such pain. Then, she explains to me that there is some "granulation tissue" left at the site that was not completely healed. Her expert opinion was to cauterize the area with silver nitrate. Assuring me that this would not hurt "at all," she proceeded to *burn* this area once a week for eleven weeks…attempting, unsuccessfully, to force it to heal. Every week there was another cauterization appointment… I began to refer to these as my "torture treatments," because the pain was intolerable. I remember that I became more and more ill as the weeks went on. I also recall crying uncontrollably from the excruciating pain I was enduring… from, you know…what wasn't supposed to hurt …

"*at all.*"

Had she *bothered* to try to figure out *why* it was so painful for me, especially after knowing what had happened during the surgery, she could have saved me a lot of misery and her insurance company a lot of money. But no…she chose to conceal this fact. I went on feeling sick and getting worse as the deadly infection aggressively sought to kill me. Basically, she was trying to cover her ass with my life. What just *kills* me looking back, is that I probably wouldn't have even sued the shit out of her if she would have just come to me and TOLD me what happened so we could find it and fix it. Shit happens. What

SHE was doing was letting me die, for fuck's sake. Okay, sorry…I got a little carried away. Back to the story…

This was a difficult time for me also due to the fact that it was what my family nicknamed *"the mad season"* at work (swimming season), and I was multi-tasking like a crazy woman while dealing with Dr. …oh, let's call her "Dr. Mengala," shall we? It is more polite than Dr. Bitch Death.

My husband and I do pools and all that they entail. His name is Dan, mine is Anna, and together we are Danna Pools Inc. Currently, we are treading water owning a successful in-ground pool business, huge warehouse and all that goes with it thanks to Dr. Mengala's insurance company and the awesome judge who presided over my trial. However, I have spent the last twenty years in and out of surgeries and treatments. Each time I persevered and thought that I had overcome my disabilities, something else occurred, and I would be diagnosed with something new.

Back then though, in 1999, we were working on both above-ground as well as in-ground pools. Having just taken the leap from working out of our basement to occupying a decent-sized rental store front in the heart of Bensenville, a suburb of Chicago near O'Hare airport, where we sold above-ground pools, pool chemicals, toys, parts, and even bathing suits. We were hoping that the retail end of the industry would help supplement the sketchy income of a seasonal construction-based business in Chicago.

Since 1991, Dan and I were operating solely from our home, enjoying the conveniences of self-employment. At the time, our two boys were about to turn ten and twelve which necessitated flexible hours due to the sheer amount of extra-curriculum activities they were involved in. I was still selling real estate, running the storefront as well as the "office," which at that time was merely a messy desk in the back room with a PC and a copy machine. I volunteered constantly for school needs and substitute taught there as well, having my ECE degree and certificate current still at the time. Although we had little time for anything else, we scurried from the boys' baseball games, to *my* baseball games, back and forth to the shop, and scampered to make it to school and social functions. Life was very busy. Sweet…but brimming with obligations. Dan and I would go through the boys' back packs each Friday with our hopes high that there would be at least *one* evening free that coming week. Although usually disappointed, we made the best of it and tried our hardest to keep up with our commitments.

As the season of 1999 started up, I was looking forward to a planned road trip with my two best friends in September. We had decided to bring some much-needed supplies to the Pine Ridge Indian Reservation in South Dakota and make it one badass adventure to remember at the same time. I have some precious friends, one who is more like a sister, whom I hadn't seen in years that live on the reservation. All of us loved to ride horses which she and her then husband, Bamm Brewer, had in abundance. Although we didn't get to see each other very often, Sissy and I, when we did, we would cry like babies to part ways. Peggy, my local BFF since second grade, owned an old RV that we transformed into what we referred to as our "peace train," complete with live flowers and tie-dyed curtains. Demi, my amazing college buddy and spiritual soul sister, was to fly in from Arizona to join us. The plan was to load up with books, blankets, clothes, and food for the needy on the reservation, meet up with another friend, Dani, at the heritage center to drop it off, and then to just relax and ride horses for a week or so…my personal version of heaven. All I needed was to get through the party, the season, and the damn surgery.

Surprisingly, I remember the day before the surgery quite clearly. So many things are fuzzy and fractured, but most of the day before the first surgery is crystal clear. Perhaps because it was the last day of my life as I had come to know it…it certainly wasn't because it was the worst of it. The hysterectomy was a cake walk compared to what I was about to go through; however, it was the beginning of the end. The first domino to fall, the reason for everything else that occurred and is still, to this very *day*, occurring.

On my mind the night before the hysterectomy was the fact that I was to report to the hospital early the next morning and that I was to go without food or water (NPO) at midnight. I was laden with worry over how the business would fare while I would be away, so I was frantically doing some last-minute paperwork at the shop. I was leaving post-it notes everywhere with comments and instructions. "Don't forget *this*." "Make sure you do *that*."

Many of my customers seemed to somehow become my *friends*, and vice versa; I don't really know why…and so there were always people coming and going regardless of my alleged business hours. People enjoyed sticking around chatting when they came in for chemicals and other necessities for their pools and friends just liked to hang out after work. I would leave the door propped open for the breeze and sometimes new customers would walk in a tad confused.

"Hello? Are you guys open?" was the usual question

"Hi! Come on in! Not really open, but I will sell you what you need" was my usual response. I guess I just answered my own question. *That* was how customers and friends would meet and jump into the "hanging out at Danna Pools after work" club with both feet. I must admit, we had a pretty awesome group of people. We laughed loudly and shared our funny stories as I tended to the stragglers.

This particular evening, May19th 1999, the weather was beautiful and about six of us sat around talking and sipping beers… a perfectly refreshing breeze wafted in from the open front door to the propped open back one. My boys were doing their homework on a folding table I had set up in the back room, laughing as the wind blew their papers away. We joined them in their laughter as they dramatically chased their homework around.

I had planned to do so many things before the surgery. Most of it was getting done and I was working on the rest when Peggy, my best friend, teased, "So…are we NOT going out for your birthday this weekend? No drinking, dancing, or partying?! This is a first!"

I laughed looking up from my stack and reminded her, "Surgery tomorrow."

She chuckled and cracked a joke about me being the only woman she knew who wanted a hysterectomy for her birthday.

"It's not like I have a choice, Peg. If I did, I would already be in Vegas by now, bleeding like a stuck pig," I told her.

We both laughed at my not-so-funny menstrual issues.

After being asked if I wanted Peggy to come to the hospital, I explained that Dan was taking me and that my sister Mikki would be there to wait with him; I thanked her for the kind offer but declined. I told her Mikki would call her afterwards.

We got a little raucous that night and stayed just a bit longer than I had planned. The kids had school the next day, and I had to stop eating and/or drinking at midnight for the procedure, so I pulled the plug on our soirée and *dragged* the kids out of there to leave. My youngest was completely blown away about the fact that I was going to get "sliced open" in the morning. He was obsessed with worry about me waking up in the middle of it. Now that I think of it, both of my boys seemed oddly uncomfortable with the whole thing, which was weird due to the fact that they were still pretty young.

"Can they video tape it so I can see it later, Momma?" my youngest asked me…completely serious.

"Good Lord, Cole…now why on *Earth* would you want to see *that?*" I asked him.

"Blood and guts!" he gruesomely announced.

This was 1999…not so much blood and guts to be found for the poor kid, as gory video games may have existed; however, they were few and far between and definitely not allowed… hell, I wouldn't even let them watch the frigging *Simpsons* yet.

The boys protested as I herded them into the car. Jesse my eldest was of course, intensely cynical…

"Mom? Just so you know, research shows that post-surgical infection is a very real threat," he stated.

"Yes, Baby, I am aware" was my answer.

The boys were still telling tabloid headline stories about crazy surgical mistakes as I pulled into our driveway, commenting to nobody in particular about the yard work that needed to be caught up on. My boys were finishing my sentences as I did this, using their shrill "mom voice" which annoyed the shit out of me. They were out of the car as soon as I put it into park, rushing off to the gate to the back yard. Customarily, I waited for Dan's truck to pull in behind me before trying to carry in all my necessary nonsense. There were binders, loose files, half empty coffee cups, trash, and all of that which had ac-companied my children *to* the car, but never left *with* them as they exited. I could usually be heard hollering the *"Hey, help me with this stuff"* cry of the weary Mom; however, their Father was pulling in, so I decided against it. My mind wandered, and I thought,

This surgery is no big deal, Anna. What are you so worried about? Think of it as a sort of vacation…

My private conversation with myself was interrupted by the sound of my husband's voice.…

"Here, give me… *stuff*" he told me as I was already handing him backpacks, empty wrappers, and other "stuff" and he asked me, "Why are you so worried?"

"I'm not" was my reply

"Really?" he mockingly asked adding

"Then why did you just hand me the tire gauge?"

Speaking over each other we said:

Me: "Oh, give me that back."

Him: "I don't know why you even *have* a tire gauge!"

Stopping, I looked at him and asked, "Wait, what?"

Dan held up the tire gauge and said, "Seriously, do you even know what to *do* with this?"

"Yep" was my answer as I snatched it from his hand.

I shoved it into the glove compartment and told him, "I put it in there!"

Dan rolled his eyes; I snickered and then out of nowhere came a shriek, "MOOOOOOOOOOOOOOOOOOOM!"

I bolted out of my car and hustled to the garage door, leaving everything as it was. As I opened the garage door into the house, my beautiful, long-haired German Shepard was, as usual, clamoring for my attention. I kissed him, petted him, and told him to calm down. I zipped to where the scream came from. I saw Cole on the stairs holding a hockey stick over his brother's head.

"Cole!" I screamed.

He only paused briefly as he called over his shoulder, "Dad said anything is fair in tormentuation!"

Jesse jumped at the chance to escape, with his brother close behind, minus the hockey stick which I held in my hand.

I looked back at my husband quizzically… he explained, "I said, 'all's fair in love and torment.'"

I cocked my head and gave him "the look." Heading up the stairs after Cole, I heard my husband say under his breath, "Little traitor."

Rolling my eyes, I asked him to order a pizza and added that I am *so not* cooking tonight.

After dealing with the mini-man civil war, I herded my little soldiers upstairs for a family meeting. Once I had them settled, I told them that their father had ordered a pizza. I waited for the celebration between them to be over, then I explained to them that tomorrow they must take the bus home from school as opposed to walking to the shop.

"You must remember." I told them. "I will *not* be able to come get you guys if you space out. I am going to be resting in my bed when you get home. Jesse, I will give you a key, so I won't have to get up to open the door."

Of course, my younger son, Cole whined in protest, "Why does *he* always get to hold the key?!"

I told him the same thing I said to him *every* time a key was needed, "He is the oldest, honey."

Jesse gave him a "ha-ha" look and patted him on the top of the head like a dog.

"Jes, cut it out" I warned him.

"Don't make me give him that hockey stick back!"

After a thought, I added as they hurried away, "Boys! Feed Maxx!"

After making sure they had no questions about the next day, I checked their homework and allowed them to go play. Dan was doing the dishes when I came into the kitchen.

"Hey, you," I greeted him, adding, "I will do those; come sit down a minute."

"Almost done," he told me, which was *his* go-to response whenever I offered to do what he was already doing.

The pizza seemed to take forever to get there. The dinner conversation was animated as the boys took turns interrupting each other about their day. I was uncharacteristically quiet. Deep in thought, I tried to listen as Dan managed to get a few sentences in edgewise, "You guys need to let your Mother rest tomorrow after school," he told them.

"You are to come home, get your homework done, and *then* you may play. No fighting, I mean it. Make sure you check on your mom; she is having a procedure done…"

Jesse interrupted, "It's a SURGERY, Dad." He said *surgery* as if it were three words.

"Yes," Dan continued, "She is having *surgery* and will need a lot of rest afterwards. I want you guys to call my cell phone when you get home if I'm not still or already here."

Cole had been playing with his pizza…picking off anything on it and making a mess. His brother looked at him and said, "Looks like a *sur-ger-y* on your plate!"

We all laughed heartily. I sent the boys to wash up, brush their teeth, and told them I would come tuck them in.

"Please, don't drag ass boys; it's late"

I called to them as they reluctantly shuffled off to prepare for bed.

When I could hear that they were in the room, still messing around, I went in and told them to bed down. Each night I sat on their respective beds, talking for a few minutes. Everything was always a competition with these two, and I could never remember whose bed I was supposed to hit up first, so I asked, "Who's turn is it tonight?"

Cole announced proudly… "Mine!", so I ambled over to his bed.

He jumped in and got cozy as I fixed his covers around him.

"Prayers, please," I said, and I listened to hear him pray. It was the usual prayer; however, he added a twist at the end.

"Please let Mama live through her surgery, because our birthday party is coming up!"

Stifling a laugh, I waited until he was done asking God to bless the family, all of the animals, and make the sign of the cross before I gently explained to him, "Sweetie, I am going to be *just fine!*"

Convinced, he kissed me, hugged me for what seemed to be a little longer than usual, smiled, and got into his "sleeping position." I looked down at him for just a few seconds before I squeezed his arm under the covers bent to give him another kiss and then moved to his brother's bed who was paging through a comic book.

I approached him; Jesse handed me the comic book, and I smiled as I put it in his drawer. I then told him to scoot over, and I sat down on his bed. I looked at my boy and smiled.

"They do these kinds of surgeries everyday" I told him. Adding, "It's actually quite common. There is almost no risk!"

"I know; I looked it up at school," he said, smiling back. "Just don't get a infection," he said.

I corrected him, "It's *an* infection." He rolled his eyes. "I hear you, Jesse. Now, prayers"

He said his nightly prayers much too quickly, but like his brother, he added a little something about keeping me safe, without the birthday party comment.

I looked at him long and hard as I tucked him in. Jesse liked the "taco tucking" which, for all of you who do NOT know, is the process of a swaddle-type tucking in at all areas. It is more like a burrito, but we called it taco tucking. I kissed and hugged him. I liked how his hug lingered. After the "I love yous" and "goodnights" and a couple of "Mom?"s with answers, I shut the door and jumped in the shower. Dan was already in bed by the time I climbed in.

I thought he was sleeping but he turned to me and asked, "You didn't eat or drink anything?"

To which I shook my head no. He opened the covers and motioned me closer, and I fell asleep in his arms. Maxx, our dog, snuck up on the bed to spoon with us.

Maxximus had some issues in the beginning… he was high strung and extremely paranoid. There were times when he just didn't *like* some random person who was around. I had rules and needed for him to distinguish right from wrong. As appreciative as I was for his protection, I couldn't let him go around biting everyone he didn't like! The two of us were learning to trust one another as we attempted to work out our issues. A couple of times we really "went at it." Just us, though. My hands and his dodge and weave moves. He would bark and growl at me, and I never let him scare me as to establish dominancy. It was a strange combination of training a horse and a dog at the same time. Like I said, he was HUGE! We both got through it with only minor injuries.

Maxx was introduced to the family when an acquaintance stopped by asking where to go to "put a dog down." I remember I was doing the dishes when he asked us. I hadn't been paying too much attention, but I totally heard THAT!

"What dog?! WHY!?" I was appalled.

The guy explained that the dog was not trainable, and he tried to bite everyone. He also explained that when they got their *new* puppy, Maxx (the dog in question), was put in a small room for 24/7 with no attention and very little room to walk around. I was apoplectic. Roy had two boys, just like us. He would purchase pets excessively, never taking proper care of them. I had seen numerous dead pet graves in his yard. These people were like animal serial killers. I found a dried-up turtle once; I have no idea how long the poor thing went without water. A flash memory of the dead turtle, shell down graced my mental imagery, but I shoved it away quickly, dried my hands and adamantly said,

"Bring that dog in here,"

Roy was holding him back severely with a choker collar as Maxx pulled and tried to get away. The sound coming from him was heartbreaking. It resembled the kind of howling you would hear on a bigfoot documentary.

"Let go of him, Roy," I told him, although Roy is not his real name.

"Anna, are you *sure?*" He was hesitant.

I raised my voice as I told him, "Let go of the dog, damnit, before he strangles himself to death!"

That dog ran throughout my house so fast that it was difficult to see what he looked like. He was huge with beautiful colors throughout his long body. Mostly cocoa brown, but areas of white and black as well. He was ripping up carpet chunks with his untrimmed nails by doing laps around the great room wall, barely missing tables and, surprisingly, not knocking anything over. I opened the back sliding-glass door, and he *flew out*, scantily pausing at the deck to access the yard. He ran and ran until he could run no more. Finally, after exhausting himself, he lay on the deck, panting. I put some water in front of him, and he drank desperately, slobbering it everywhere. I was getting splashed; however, I didn't mind… I was finally able to get a good look at him. He was beautiful. Mostly German shepherd with some collie in him which gave him a full, soft, long-haired mane around his neck. He reminded me of the cowardly lion from Wizard of Oz. He was inordinately large; however, he was just over a year old without an ounce of fat on him. I watched him lap up the water; he kept looking up at me to be sure I was still there. I reached out to this beautiful creature and looked into his big dark eyes. With my hand held out I told him,   "Don't bite me."

He sniffed my hand before licking it with his wet, massive, lolling tongue. He bent closer to lick my face, and we instantly connected. I knew right then that we have a new dog.

Bite people? I thought to myself, *I call Bullshit.*

However, I was wrong. He *did* bite people. A few unlucky relatives and friends were on the receiving end of his judgement. Maxx would nip the fingers of some and would even *leap* at those who he decided he *really* didn't like. This was not his way with everyone. He adored my sisters, especially Mikki and he worshipped the boys. However, there were many times when Maxx would jump to "protect" us when we were simply playing around. I deduced that this behavior must have come from his abuse and neglect while with "Roy's" family. I finally accepted the fact that he would need to be completely re-trained.

After making the decision to keep the dog, Maxx quickly blended into our family perfectly. He was quite partial to me; however, he loved the entire family passionately. After some hard work, he evolved into the best dog I have ever had. He followed me everywhere I went like a shadow, which was what Dan would call him, "shadow," teasingly.

Re-training Maxx was similar to working with a "green-broke" horse. Green-broke is a term used for a horse that either wasn't finished with training or was trained improperly. It amazed me how intelligent he was, how he could sense my emotions *and* how I felt physically. When the pain was intense, or the nausea devastating, he knew and comforted me. Although he was freakishly protective of us, he could be the sweetest and most loving dog. God help anyone who tried to hurt us, though! We would be arguing on the phone at someone, and he would look at the phone and growl. When the boys were fighting, which was almost always, he would come to me and whine until I intervened. I had to be careful with my feelings. He picked up on how I felt and treated people accordingly. He didn't like who I didn't care for, and he scared the shit out of some people at times, but oh, how I loved that dog. When he passed away, I mourned more intensely than I have for most *humans*.

Not long after adopting Maxx, I was throwing one of my many impromptu "after the boys' baseball game everyone comes to my house" parties, and we had some newbies that night. I won't mention her name, but one baseball mom was on Maxx's shit list immediately, and I knew it. There was *something* about this woman that he *hated*; I do not know what, but I could tell he wanted to bite her. I tried to make peace, although I didn't really *know* this woman very well, and Maxx persisted. I spoke to her, encouraging her to be careful around him. I asked her to not approach him. I also kept switching Maxx from indoors to outdoors, trying to keep distance between the two of them. Most of those present that evening knew and *loved* Maxx, so someone must have let him out when I wasn't paying attention. I caught it right away and went out there…

What happened next was insane! A host of our big *manly* friends were out on our deck, and the woman Maxx disliked was standing near them on the second level. I noticed Maxx looking at her … in that *way* he had. Not wanting an incident, I called his name, and he came towards me. Now Maxx had to *pass* her to get to me, and he turned to look back at her after catching her scent going by, and if I didn't *see* it happen, I never would have believed it, but **she growled at him!** My eyes went wide, and my mouth dropped open…. she looked so evil that it scared the shit out of *me*! Maxx had turned around, and suddenly, he was in midair trying to leap all the way over to her, but I leaped as well and caught him by the butt. I pulled back on him, getting a better grasp until I could throw him in the basement for one of our one on one beating meetings. What shocked me more than *anything* though was that not one man jumped in to help me! They watched in fright while I wrestled Maxx as he thrashed, growling, both of us rolling down the last tier of the deck to get to the basement where we duked it out. The only person brave enough to even get *involved* was my BFF Peggy. Maxx knew her like another Mom...she opened the basement door as I bear hugged him and threw him the laundry room. Dan had been on a beer run, and when he returned to the ass-end of the drama, he was busting balls *bad* at his friends for not helping "a one-hundred-pound woman against a one-hundred-pound animal." It was funny, because I heard a couple of comments from the motley crew of alleged macho men as Maxx and I spilled into the laundry room...

Damn. Check that out; she's crazy man!

Mm-mmm, no way, man.

...and one long scream that sounded more like a ten-year-old Girl Scout than a 220-pound grown-ass man.

It wasn't long before Maxx and I become like two peas in a pod. He would carry himself a certain way or stare at someone in a particular way, and I would KNOW that we had a problem. During these circumstances, I would put him in my room. It got to the point to where he would just go to my room on his *own* when certain people came over. Making himself scarce around certain friends that, for one reason or another, he did not care for. I should have trusted his judgement...each "friend" he disliked at one point or another proved to be disingenuous or worse. I was friends with a woman who I knew in grade school, her son being the same age as Jesse and his best friend for years. I thought it was a normal friendship; she had a few annoying quirks, but I try to accept people for who they are. Well, Maxx hated her. It turns out that, after years of hanging out together, I caught her *spitting in my coffee!* Who does that?! Sensing something was off, I placed some cameras around my home and found that she also stole from me, and even worse, she did some disgusting and confounding things to my personal possessions (toothbrushes, etc.) I won't even go there. Let's just say she is a very sick individual who needs an entire *team* of therapists. She hid her insanity cunningly and fooled me for a while, but she couldn't fool Maxx. He always eyed her suspiciously. I believe he smelled her resentment, or her bat-shit craziness. I'm just glad that I *saw* the ugly brown…*whatever it was*, on my toothbrush and never used it. I was disgusted, and ever since then, to this *day*, I do not keep my toothbrush in the bathroom anymore.

Maxx was an integral part of my healing; we spent endless hours together comforting each other. We had built a foundation of trust and friendship, and it didn't take him long to become the world's greatest dog I ever had. He barely left my side, and I mourn him fiercely still to this day. When I was very sick, if I wasn't in the hospital, I was in bed at home; Maxx was always with me. As an inpatient, friends would sneak him up to see me! He was so smart that he *knew* to be low key and ninja like.

Although the years of dealing with the many surgeries I incurred due to Mengala's neglect, the organ damage, nerve damage and, *well all of it* was horrific, my pets brought me comfort, company, and kept me busy. We had quite the diverse crew of animals at our home!

My sister Mikki had given my boys an iguana when they were young. "Liz" was her name. Dan constructed her a custom cage (which she was usually out of), and it was so big that it took up half of the great room. It was a beautiful handmade lizard mansion constructed of plexiglass and oak with a screen top for her lights. Liz grew to be six feet long and an excellent pet. She loved to swim and be held. I didn't feed her crickets or bugs; she was a vegetarian, as I am, and she loved her high calcium, low phosphorane greens and berries. I put a cricket in there with her once, just to see what would occur, and she made friends with it. It would sit on her head and sing. I am not sure what happened to that cricket, but Liz was with us for fourteen years. One of her favorite "haunts" to the horror of a few "popped-in gotta pee" friends was the top of the shower curtain in the upstairs bathroom. It happened twice actually. The first time it was Peggy, and I heard her cooing Liz, "Oh, Hi, Liz! Such a pretty girl."

The second time was hilarious…I was doing paperwork at my dining room table, and my sweet, fun, *frantic* friend Renee burst through the door saying she had to pee so bad and went running into my bathroom. It took a second but then she shrieked, "Anna! There's a dinosaur in here!"

I told her, "Don't scream, Renee! You will scare her!"

She was in dismay as she said, "You're worried about *me* scaring *her?!*"

Liz was very gentle and laid back. She was litter box/water trained, so she wasn't exactly low maintenance. The cage needed to be cleaned constantly, and she needed to be sprayed with water many times a day. She had her own little, quirky personality, and we loved her just as much as we loved all of our animals. When she wanted to get out, she would simply pop the screen with her head and climb out. Mostly she would lay in the bay window of my great room, soaking up rays of sunshine, but she also loved to go outside. Liz would hold her head high and revel in the feeling of the grass and the wind out in the yard. The problem was that, when she was out there, she was perfectly camouflaged. Frighteningly, we lost track of her a few times. She could be quite quick when she tried to be! On one occasion, I remember the whole neighborhood was looking for her, the local children organized a search and rescue mission. Liz was on a shelf in our garage the ENTIRE time. Another escape sent my husband up a significantly large tree to fetch her. Good times.

Our bird liked to hang out in the lizard cage, right on her *head*. Yes, a bird too…we acquired a small tropical love bird we named Pedro.

While working on a new house build in 1987, Dan kept hearing a strange squawk. The bird then began dive-bombing Dan, landing on him, squawking, and flying away…over and over until finally he landed on Dan's shoulder and stayed there until I came to the job site from home (more accurately from the pet shop) with a cage and food. He was gorgeous. Although he was mostly green and yellow, when he spread his wings there was a beautiful blue phoenix marking on his back. I deduced that he must have gotten away from a home, because when he saw the cage, he went directly for it. Hungrily inhaling the food, he sat on its small wooden swing, trembling. I, of course, took him back to my house.

I watched the classifieds, the old school internet, for weeks, and no one was looking for him, so we absorbed him into our family. Then there was our Mystic. She was a rescue cat that I justified keeping by the fact that many of the mice Jesse was breeding for his baby python (Monty) had gone loose and were literally swinging from the bird cage looking for food in there. It was crazy. I loved it though, even the chaos. I was living the best days of my life. I look back now, smile and cry at the memories. Currently, it is 2019 as I write this… Mystic just passed away at twenty-one years old, and we all miss her terribly. I cannot help but be angry when I think of the great life I had going and how Doctor Mengala basically murdered it. Just when I thought we had it all figured out…wham, she kicks my legs right out from under me. It is difficult to speculate how *different* my life would be right now, the things we could have accomplished if she hadn't ruined everything…

The morning of the hysterectomy I had a strange feeling of impending doom. This, I kept to myself, writing it off as pre-surgical jitters. Looking back, I SO wish I hadn't.

It was such a hectic morning, throwing me out of my daily routine. The boys' bus picked them up on the corner directly in front of our home every morning, but not until 8:00 A.M., and Dan and I needed to leave earlier. After going over the rules far too many times, I *almost* felt secure that they would be fine on their own. They *are* almost twelve and ten years old after all. Many thoughts raced through my mind…

Should I have driven them? Should I wait till the bus comes and be late for the surgical check in?

Maybe we could do this whole surgery thing another time…

I often wonder if these thoughts were my window to jump out of, but at the time, I didn't realize it. If I had known what was about to be put in motion, I would never have shown up to the hospital that day.

In hindsight, there are things about the morning of the first of far too many surgeries that stand out to me now. Why hadn't I *overthought* them as I did most *everything else in my life?* Even now, I remember feeling that something was not quite right. Strange experiences were occurring. Weird little things out of the ordinary, indicating that I was missing something. It was a feeling as though there was *something* that I had *forgotten*…that nagging thought that sits just outside your realm of comprehension. Did I *know* somehow that this was to be the first domino to fall? Thinking back, Van Morrison's hit song "Domino" always pops into my head…

Lord have mercy, I said, OH, oh, dominooo

As we scrambled to get out the door, Maxx paced whining. He was circling me and, due to his size, almost caused me to fall. He usually only did this when we were packing suitcases which we were *not*, and I wondered if he was trying to tell me something. I petted and cooed him before I left. I told him we would be back soon. Nothing seemed to calm him down. I was curious as to why he would act such a way, but I blew it off. Now I theorize that even the *dog* seemed to sense that I shouldn't go that day.

I glanced at Dan in the car on the way to the hospital. He said, "What, babe? You're going to be fine!"

"I know" was what I said, but not how I felt …and he sensed it.

That feeling…just out of brain shot was baffling me. In my head, I was going over a million different things: the kids, the business, the batting order of the softball team, and Maxx's behavior. Although I had planned meticulously, I kept thinking *something* was off. Just not right.

The best example of these strange experiences…what I now consider to be my *gut* trying to tell me to bolt would be the discussion Dan and I had with my sister Mikki in the presurgical room mere minutes before the start of the surgery.

When she had checked in to be with Dan and I, my sister Mikki actually *spoke* to the doctor who was to perform my surgery. I can still remember the confused look on her face when she tried explaining why she wasn't very… for lack of a better term, *impressed* with her. She said that while speaking to the doctor, her lab coat had pulled back, revealing her clothing underneath. She was wearing a long, sequined ball gown. Surprised, yet a bit confused, my sister asked her if she was going to an exciting black-tie event right after surgery, only to be told by the doctor, "Oh no…" and then the doctor laughed in a strange way and added, "I *always* operate in this! I just *love* the way it feels!" She opened her lab coat and swirled around to model for her. My sister was shocked to say the least, and she told Dan and I all about it.

Like my sister, neither Dan nor I thought this to be normal. Odd looks were on *all* our faces as we tried to find a reason for this to have been an ordinary thing to say…and to *do*. Nothing came to mind. I should have sprinted for the door right then and there. Dan and I stared wide eyed at my sister upon hearing her story, and I asked her, "Mikki? What *color* is the dress?"

She looked at me as if she had just swallowed something *ugly*. "Red...*blood red*" was what she said

"Oh, that's just perfect," I said sarcastically.

But what if…

My mind *raced* with revolting possibilities. Little did I know, *then*, that her sexy red sequin dress losing some bling in my body would be the least of my post-surgical concerns.

Please let those sequins be sewn tightly though, I remember thinking.

Upon receiving whatever the nurse pushed through my IV, I compliantly nodded off to never-neverland. My last thought was that of my doctor, shimmering gloriously in red and dancing...on top of my naked, surgically prepped *body*. The song she was dancing to was heavy metal. She was singing loudly off key as she danced, similar to "Elaine" in Seinfeld, and sequins were flying everywhere.

It was…festively frightening.

I will have to admit to a certain level of *collusion* where the hysterectomy was concerned. I was told it was necessary… lifesaving even. I was also told that I would no longer have a monthly period which sounded great to me. The doctor assured me that I would be, and these are her words verbatim, "Fine! Walking around and back to your old self a week later."

While planning for the surgery, the timing was very important to me, because one week after the hysterectomy, *exactly…* was a very special event. The boys' big birthday bash.

I had planned the boys' yearly birthday bash early that season. Jesse was turning twelve and Cole, ten. Since their birthdays, although two years apart, were only two weeks from the other, I would usually throw one big party for both each year. This year the boys wanted the party to have a camping theme … complete with a big bonfire and tents in the backyard, filled with their friends.

Many of their friends were mutual, since they were the children of the people Dan and I would hang around with, and the children of our family members… although that was changing. As they got older, the boys were finding their own friends. The age difference between them being both a curse and a blessing. The friends they made often becoming warring factions as well as trusted allies. The politics of growing up teaching them lessons they would need later in life. I often wonder how different my sons' lives would be had none of the medical mayhem occurred.

I can still hear Dr. Mengala telling me that I would be, "Fine, back to my old self again in a week".

What is tragically ironic is that I have *never* felt like my "old self" since the hysterectomy…not once. She should have just used a *gun* and been humane about killing me instead of the havoc she wreaked upon my life, my body and the emotions of my husband and children. It is quite surreal, to say the least, knowing that one situation changed my life that drastically.

The first *mention* of "the surgery" was less than two weeks prior to its occurrence. It doesn't matter how many surgeries I go through or their severity… after twenty-six surgeries, the first hysterectomy will always be "the" surgery to me. It wasn't my first; it *surely* wasn't the worst, but it started *everything. Nothing was ever the same again.*

OH, Ohhhhh, dominooooo Roll me over, Romeo… ♪

There you go. Lord have mercy! I said Oh… Oh…. Oh, domino ♪

In the surgical waiting room, my sister Mikki was worried. They told her that the hysterectomy would take forty-five minutes and that I would be in recovery for maybe half of an hour or so. It had been three hours and counting. She was concerned that something may have gone wrong… if only she *knew.*

Right about then, in the OR, Dr. Mengala and her not-so-secret lover were arguing about whose *fault* it was that my fallopian tube had disappeared from sight. The evil she doctor was scraping around furiously inside my body looking for it despite her lover's protests, telling her that she would cause even *more* problems by doing so. Or so he claimed through deposition.

When the fourth hour came, the distracted, frustrated doctor tossed *something* in a stainless-steel operating room container and said, "There. *There* it is."

The surgical nurse she handed it to eyed it suspiciously, seeing nothing but bloody tissue. She caught the eye of a fellow OR nurse and slightly motioned her over to see the "sample" she held. They both looked at it and then at each other. The first nurse whispers to her comrade…"She is just going to give up on finding it?!"

All she received in response was a shrug of the other nurse's shoulders and a wide-eyed glare.

Here... let *me* answer that one for you ...

Yes. She was just going to give up on finding it. She was going to pretend as if everything went fine. When I woke up in recovery after the hysterectomy, I was told that everything went great and that I would be feeling better soon. I was quite relieved, given that it was only seven days from the big birthday party for my boys.

Now, I am a very upbeat, positive person with a high pain tolerance. I also had a burning passion to return to my awesome life. Despite having the right attitude, one week later, I was far from "my old self." Not only did I NOT feel better each day, I actually felt WORSE. The pain and discomfort were beyond frustrating. With each passing day, I felt more and more sick. Seven days after the hysterectomy, the day of the big party, I spiked a fever of 103 degrees and felt as though I were dying from nausea and internal pain.

My husband frantically called the doctor who was vacationing overseas. She was made *well aware* of the facts. My fever, my condition, and all of the *tell-tale* signs that I had acquired a raging infection; however, she did nothing about it. She sent me to the ER a couple of times but never ordered any blood cultures; all they did was fill me with fluids, pain medicine, and brought down the fever. In hindsight, I'm astonished that neither of the attending ER doctors took blood cultures, which is practically *standard* that soon after a major surgery. We never found proof that she *discouraged* these lifesaving ideas; however, we DID prove that she didn't order any. Had she done so, my story would have ended here. I would have been prescribed a "super drug" oral antibiotic, and I probably never would have needed heart surgery. I don't know *what* she was thinking. All I can come up with is that she wanted me to die, just go away. *Many* were the times I sat on her examination table post-surgically and not *once* did she check my temp, listen to my heart, or even order any blood work. She merely examined me, announced that the tiny piece of "granulation tissue" was still unhealed, and that cauterizing it with silver nitrate was the way to go. I know *now* that she was covering her own ass. As soon as she knew that the cautery caused me great pain, she should have factored in the rogue tube. Cauterizing granulation tissue does *not* cause pain unless there is an underlying reason. Prior to the first cautery, I had asked her if the procedure would be painful, she was adamant, "Oh no!" she emphatically exclaimed, adding, "*not at all.*"

I screamed bloody murder in pain as she applied the silver nitrate, and when she was done, I was quite angry. I know *now* that the fact that the cauterizations HURT should have alerted her to the reality that there was something present at the site of cautery besides granulation tissue. Knowing that she never found the tube, she would have to be an *idiot* or *evil* not to hypothesize that it was involved in the problem. Unfortunately for all involved, she did nothing. I assume that she was concerned to alert anyone of her surgical screw up. I saw her each week after the hysterectomy, and each time, she cauterized the wound, and I screamed in pain. There were eleven cauterizations in all. It was so horrible that I began referring to them as my "torture treatments." I could not drive myself to them, because I felt so sick and weak, not to mention that I would be in tears from *pain* after the procedure she assured me wouldn't hurt "at all" and in no shape to drive home. It felt as though each appointment made me feel worse…each hurt more than the last.

Now, no one *forced* her to be a doctor. Dealing daily with human lives was her *choice*. I recall the final torture treatment like it occurred *yesterday*. I cussed loudly as the pain shot through my entire body, and I remember getting *the stink eye* from her. She furrowed her brow and said angrily, "Oh, come now! Stop that screaming!"

I was much too despondent to even *try* to defend myself. I could merely think,

Am I crazy? This pain is real! Right…?

My sister Mikki had driven me that day. She drove me often as Dan was busy handling *everything else*. When I think of how full Dan's plate was, it still astounds me that he held it all together while I slowly wasted away.

The actual act of each cauterization was quick. I attempted to ask her questions and communicate with her about how ill I felt; however, she seemed to successfully ditch me each time. On one occasion, she informed me that she would return to the exam room to listen to my questions and concerns; however, after waiting a half hour, I was told she left on an emergency. Snuck out the back door was what she did!

My sister had even stopped coming into the office with me. She would sit in the car and wait; that's how fast it would happen. That bitch would burn me and throw me out while I was in mid-sentence, trying to ask her questions. The memory of her trite, condescending statements continues to haunt me to this very day;

"You are just *fine*."

"You need to be strong and positive."

"Don't be such a baby!" was my favorite!

If I wasn't so weak and sick, I would've let her have it.

Prior to going through the final torture session, I *knew* that this was the last appointment I intended to attend. It was the eleventh cautery procedure.

My husband had told me that morning that if this cautery "didn't take," he was finding a new doctor. He had never seen me look so sick. I had never *felt* as sick. Mikki drove me to the final appointment. She stopped me as I went to get out of the car. She waited until I looked her in the eye and told me, "This is crazy. How many times is she going to *DO* this? Doesn't she see how sick you are?"

Although I agreed with her, I honestly didn't know what else to do. What kind of doctor should I go see? I was sick, confused, and weary of all of it. I merely wanted my life back. I believe I tried each time to convince myself that it would be the last appointment and that I would finally heal. I was so pathetically positive that it now pisses me off tremendously.

I almost hit the ceiling on that last cautery the pain was SO bad. I decided to discontinue the torture treatments, pump vitamins and herbal medicine into my body, meditate more, and convince myself that I was fine. I truly *had* to! The trip with my friends to deliver needed donations to the reservation was mere days away already! Peggy, Demi, and I would talk daily hashing out the plans. We were *all* looking forward to it, and I threw my attention into working out the details of the trip. I had arranged for large amounts of grocery donations from a local market, blankets and clothing from a second-hand store. I kept occupied by using any spare moment I had to organize. The "peace train" would soon be packed to the gills with food, clothes, blankets, and more, as the donations came trickling in. I couldn't *wait* to see Sissy!

Surprisingly, my half-assed holistic healing strategy seemed to be working, and I began to feel a bit better each day. The human mind is amazing. I almost felt "normal" the day that we pulled the hippie-mobile out of the driveway and headed out on our road trip. Thinking about it now, it must have been mostly adrenaline along with a lot of "mind over matter," because in reality, I was running around with an undiagnosed deadly infection.

Right about this time, maybe a week before the trip, I received an urgent call from my sister Kimberly who was in Las Vegas visiting our father.

My mother and father lived in Melrose, however, had a condo in Las Vegas where they planned to retire. They would go back and forth...well at least my mom would. Daddy was too nervous to leave his business, a small shot and beer tavern, to travel with her much. I remember that he used to call it "your mother's condo" instead of claiming it which left me thinking he didn't much care for the place. I was shocked when he had decided to stay in Vegas to *live* and sell the Melrose property once she passed, it was touching. All of us tried to fly in to check on him as much as possible. I found it romantic, because my father claimed *not* to like it there when Mom was alive and well yet, unpredictably, sold the bar and building and decided to live there year-round during her illness and after her death. He once told me that he brought her back to the condo just before she died, because it was her favorite place to be. He thought it might help her to recover. Him staying there to live, I believe, was a tribute to her and his love for her.

I was lucky growing up; my mother and father truly loved one another. We called my dad Papa. Papa was perpetually broken-hearted over the loss of our mother. Four years later, his already bad memory was starting to freak us all out. He was exhibiting the beginning signs of Alzheimer's disease. My husband and I had just been there by him for a visit in the spring, and although I noticed a decline, I felt as though he was doing alright. Kimberly went in August, and a day after she had arrived, she called me. That is how fast his relentless disease progressed. Kim told me over the phone, "I am sending Daddy home to live with you. He is unable to care for himself properly!"

Dan and I switched the "office" into Papa's room and gladly awaited his arrival. I love my dad, and I was excited to know he was coming. They just don't make them like my dad anymore. Still to this day, people approach me to tell me what a wonderful man he was. Amazing. Kind, gregarious, funny as hell, generous to a fault, and full of love for his family. He was handsome, 100 percent Italian with a killer smile. My father had a way of making people feel at ease. His humor and wit made everyone feel comfortable. His warm charm magnetically pulled you right in. He treated my mother like a queen. I used to say that he was living proof that all men aren't assholes. That was our Papa. He loved to spoil us when he could. Us girls, myself and my sisters, would as my brothers always said, "Get away with murder" growing up. He was tough on his boys but treated us girls like royalty, however, was extremely over-protective. He had come from a strict, solid, and large Abruzzese family. The only time I would get angry with my daddy was when it came down to dating. It took him until I was seventeen to allow it, and when he *finally* did, he drilled every boy who came to pick me up. He and my eldest brother, Bobby, would decide if I was allowed to go or not. It was so humiliating, and I would get much shit for it in high school. I remember one time, my date pulled up in a van, and my father sent him packing. He told me, "No vans!"

There were many "dating" rules. No vans being just one, no skirts, another. No make-up, no alluring attire, no motorcycles...and so many more that escape me now. Both of my brothers and my father would scrutinize how I looked before allowing me out. I wouldn't tolerate when Dominick, the younger of my two brothers would chime in. Bobby, my oldest brother was thirteen years older than I and more of a father figure. I was the youngest of five and often left in the care of either Mikki or Bobby. Being the "caboose," as my dad would call me, I had the hardest time getting away with *anything*. My elder siblings had schooled my parents in just about *everything* through personal experience! I laugh out loud when I remember one date. Papa asked me where I was going.

"To the movies, Papa," I answered.

"What is the name of the movie?" he asked me.

"*The Amityville Horror*," I answered.

My father's eyes widened, and he was genuinely shocked as he said, "Amy the whore? What kind of guy would take a lady to see a movie like that?!"

I screamed, "Maaaaaaaaaaaaaaaaaaa!"

As usual, my mother came in to diffuse the situation.

That is one of my *favorite* "Papa stories"; however, there are *many*. One night, my mother who usually never swore, was watching a political debate on TV and blurted out "ASSHOLE!" quite loudly.

Those of us who were present at the time were staring wide-eyed at my mother when Daddy walked in and asked her, "Are you calling me, hun?" None of us could stop laughing.

I remember when Paula, my sister's best friend, was over after school, and Daddy walked in from work and said to her, "Oh, hi, Paula! I didn't know I was here!"

He would ask my best friend, "What is your first name again, Peggy?"

He would trip over the dog and holler, "Get off of the way!" as opposed to "get *out* of the way." He would say "you want I should…" instead of "should I," and on the rare occasion that he was angry, he would abandon the English language completely for Italian. We would all holler, "English, Papa!"

When I think of my father now, I smile and feel very blessed to have had the upbringing that I complained against at the time.

Upon receiving the call from my sister Kim, I decided to use this opportunity to spend quality time with my dad as he was always busy working when I was growing up. It was horrifying to watch his sharp mind disintegrate as the evil disease progressed, but I was happy to have him with us. After a while, his conversational redundancy was constant; however, I found it sweet. Endearing even.

I made arrangements with Dan and Mikki to help with Daddy while I would be away on my road trip. He arrived two days before I left. I felt bad that I was leaving so much responsibility to Dan on his own, but there was *no way* I was missing this trip. We had mapped it out so that we would hit several reservations before ending up on Pine Ridge.

When it was "road trip time," I was stoked! My children and some of their neighborhood friends rode their bikes alongside us as I drove the HUGE RV (or "peace train," if you will) carefully through the neighborhood. Being the resident control freak of the group, I, of course, would let no one else drive. Demi and Peggy hung out of the windows waving at the kids. I was a bit less jubilant than they as I negotiated the turns and lane changes of the thirty-foot behemoth under my control. I *do* remember telling the girls after being asked how I was feeling…that as soon as I got home from this trip I was going to see a new doctor, because I just wasn't feeling right. I knew I wasn't 100 percent, but I had *no* idea that a serious and deadly infection coursed through my blood…in and out of all my vital organs.

I was far too excited about my adventure though to pay it any mind. The infection came with us on our trip like a nasty little stowaway.

Several hours later, I was just starting to get comfortable with the piece of shit camper on I 90 when I noticed she was pulling to the right rather severely. I turned down the music to talk to the girls. Like a couple of teenagers, they protested with whiney wails. I turned it back up and waited for the song to end, rolling my eyes.

"Camper is pulling hard to the right," I reported.

We drove on, a bit nervous when the RV began to make odd noises, still pulling to the right. It turned out that we had good reason to worry. Our first heart-pounding adventure occurred when the rear suspension dropped like a bomb, and I was forced to wrangle the camper to the side of the road. We were just passing a small town about a hundred miles before Des Moines, Iowa when it happened. It felt like King Kong just stepped on the back of the camper! The wheel locked itself up tightly, taking every ounce of strength I had to pull her over to the side of the road. It was dark, so I had *no idea* that the narrow shoulder I just cruised over onto *dipped* six feet down into a ravine. By all rights, we *should have* been sent careening into the void and exploding on impact, but we were incredibly lucky. We were all already freaking out when out of *nowhere* we were forcefully thrown around the camper by the velocity of an eighteen-wheeler passing inches away from us doing at least ninety miles an hour. I thought for sure we were going to roll down the incline as the camper rocked. I dove to put the hazard lights on as we continued to shake from the power of the truck that had barely missed us. I decided to go out and make sure that the hazard lights were working. First, I opened the front passenger door… well, more accurately, it opened *itself* via gravity, and it almost tossed me out as we were tilted sharply to the right. I gazed at the drop and thanked God for letting us stay on the shoulder. Instead of even *attempting* to close the door, I blocked the area by placing a tall cardboard box on the seat as a warning for anyone who forgets about the ditch. Looking around it and down, I could see a *very* narrow precipitous edge. Turning and announcing over my shoulder, I hollered, "Okay…no one goes out this door you guys!"

I heard something in response, but I needed them to be *sure*. "Seriously! If you go out THIS door, you will fall and probably break a leg. Just stay away from it completely!"

I thought I was done lecturing until I noticed the sweet, sharp smell of marijuana.

"Uum…you guys? Have you been smokin'? Because the state police are gonna stop to help us…I really don't feel like getting busted. Where is your pot? Stash it somewhere good. I will be right back, I'm going to…"

I was interrupted by another massive semi-truck almost hitting us as it flew by frighteningly close. This one blared its horn long and loud. I raised my voice sharply and told the girls, "I need to go out there and see if the hazards are even working! Just before pulling over, we had descended down a hill and now these trucks are flying over it! I need to know if they can even *see* us."

Climbing up into the driver's seat, I opened the door with all my might until I could squeeze out and drop down. Looking at the ass of the camper I could see a tiny red light blinking and was horrified to know that it was probably *invisible* to the truckers speeding over the hill. I panicked, jumped back in the camper, shut the door, and quickly addressed my friends, "Okay, you guys, LISTEN UP!"

They must have sensed my urgency, because immediately I had their full attention.

"The hazard lights are for shit! I want each of you to handle one of the interior lights and be ready to flash them on and off when I tell you to!"

Since there were only two interior light switches, I manned the brights, not quite knowing if it would help or not. I figured it couldn't hurt.

"If I tell you to get out, it is because a truck is about to hit us… jump out the side door into the ravine! You know, the one I told you to stay away from. Seriously! Right out this way!"

I motioned towards the passenger side open door.

"Whatever limbs you don't want broken, tuck in! Tuck and roll! Just like being thrown off a horse! Okay, here comes another truck! Everyone get ready! And…..BLINK! GO! On and off and on and off! Yeah, like that! Woo Hooo! Great job, you guys!"

We could see the adjustment that the truck made as he came barreling towards us.

OH, THANK GOD

It wasn't long before we were awash in the glow of blue and red police lights. I was glad to see them, yet a bit nervous about the way the camper smelled.

"Somebody *spray* something! It smells like a Grateful Dead concert in here!" I chided them adding, "Geez! How much pot did you guys *smoke?*"

I wriggled through the driver's door and met the two police officers outside.

"Hidey!" the big guy greeted me.

He was first to approach. "Is everyone okay?" He asked. After I told him what happened he affirmed that we were very lucky.

"Your rear axle dropped like a possum in a hole trap there, little lady!" Barney Fife chimed in, removing his hat and scratching his head adding,

"How in tarnation did you wrestle her to the side without going down that holla'?! That is *quite impressive!*"

Holla? Oh, Hollow…

I couldn't help myself… "Aw shucks, officer…twasn't nuthin,'" I answered, trying to keep a straight face. Big dude told us to just relax while they woke up the town tow truck owner and put flares around the camper.

A one-tow truck town, I reckon.

I looked at the tiny red hazard lights and shook my head. It was truly embarrassing how inept the emergency lights were.

I almost *stroked out* when the skinny, younger cop (very Barny Fife like) started smelling the air like a cartoon character.

SHIT, SHIT, SHIT, SHIT

He walked up to me, and I braced myself tightly as he said, "It figures you would be stuck right next to a rag weed field! HAHAW!"

I took in a large sigh of relief. Playing stupid and knowing that I was not stoned, I tilted my head and asked, "Is *that* what that smell is?"

The big guy nudged him and shook his head "no."

"Sorry, ma'am" the poor kid mustered.

"Yes, it is," explained Big dude. "It smells like…well, just like marijuana but it's a weed…"

Cutting himself off, he motioned to his partner, and suddenly they were whisper-arguing off towards their vehicle. All I heard him say at the end was… something about getting flares around the camper before it gets pulverized by an eighteen-wheeler.

I went inside and updated the girls on the situation, nearly gagging on the perfume that they had sprayed everywhere. Then I remembered what I told them…

"Okay…no more spraying. Cops are trying to get us help and don't worry about the pot smell, it isn't you guys. It seems that we ended up right next to a rag weed field."

After I told them to arrange a small version of their necessary stuff, because it looks like we may be spending the night, I did the same. Soon, we were clustered together with Big Dude and Barney Fife waiting for "the town tow truck." I cannot remember the name of the small town or the number of the population, but I am pretty sure that *all of them* were present as the camper was finally towed backwards down its main street.

The officers had told the onlookers that our plans were to bring supplies to the needy. The villagers were so impressed that, the next morning, most of them showed up to help us move everything from the disabled peace train into the discounted van we rented with their help to continue the trip. By 11:00 A.M., we were back on the road no worse for wear. Of course, I was driving.

The rest of the trip went pretty much as planned. It ended up being one of the most amazing trips of my life. One of those memories that actually knock the wind out of you to recall, putting a smile on your face for the rest of the day, generating, not just memories, but strong feelings as well. Clear thoughts of the adventures, laughter, tears, and awe.

I did an incredible amount of driving, but I also did a lot of horseback riding through open land with no restrictions…no "speed limit" except for the care of the horse and myself. Bamm and Sissy would teach me the Lakota ways and I have never felt more "at home" while away as I did at Bamm and Sissy's ranch. They have a large amount of land, a majestic herd of buffalo and countless beautiful horses! It is a very special feeling when you "open up" a fast horse, allowing her to run as fast as she chooses. It's as if you are *flying!* You and your horse are moving together as one, in complete and total sync with each other. Melting into the rhythm of her powerful body beneath me as we flew… To me, that was *heaven*. That trip was amazing. There were no protests going on for once and Sis had taken some days off of work. We would take the horses into town if we wanted to, tying them up to the shopping cart structure. We spent quiet nights up on the hill on Bamm's land and saw more stars than you can imagine. Ginger, one of my favorite of Bamm's horses would actually sneak half into my tent or teepee at night when we slept out there! Oh, those summer nights on the Ridge… heavy sigh. The night sky was a large part of the pull I felt towards Pine Ridge. I love the way you can hardly see any space between the stars. In Chicago, I am lucky to catch site of the big dipper…some nights I can't even see a single star, yet on the Ridge…they ruled the heavens. Staring up at the sky, day and night, whether in Chicago or Pine Ridge, is a love of mine. It is where I got my nickname "Skye" from my "brother" Tom Poor Bear years before.

I had met Tom at a large powwow in Chicago when I was a teenager and spent the entire weekend talking to him. There was an instant connection between the two of us, and it is how I ended up starting to go to Pine Ridge. Upon seeing me on the rez a few times and revisiting when I protested at his Camp Justice, Tom decided to do me the great honor of asking me to become his adopted sister and, in doing so, gave me an Indian name. "She stares at the Sky" or…Skye. In Lakota it is *Mahpiya tho*; however, Tom often called me *Pispiza*, which means prairie dog. He said I was always digging in my stuff and popping my head up like a prairie dog pops in and out of the earth. He's right; I was always digging in my bag popping up, saying things like, "I can't find my socks!" or "Hold on I just need to grab something."

To this day, "Skye" is the only name my American Indian family addresses me as. I am more than fine with that. Everyone in my life is aware of it and has had no complaint either. Of course, I need to explain it at times, but I am still honored to have been asked and each time I explain, there is a lump in my throat.

An interesting occurrence on the trip; at the *wopila* ceremony (a Lakota Thank You event), I stood in line to receive gifts from the tribe, and an elder approached me. After handing me the blanket she had made me, she touched my hand and stopped the slow-moving line.

"Skye, you are ill," she told me.

"Oh no, Grandmother," I explained. "I am just tired."

The old woman looked deep into my eyes and emphatically repeated, "Skye, you are ill, my dear."

I smiled at her curiously. On her face was a concerned look.

Sissy was next to me accepting gifts and she leaned in saying quietly, "Maybe she means *mentally*, Skye."

I shoved her in retaliation, both of us laughing, and I soon forgot all about it. I mentioned it later to my brother Tom, and he suggested I see a doctor when I returned to the city.

"Grandmother knows," he told me with a concerned look on his face.

My adoptive brother Tom Poor Bear is now the vice-president of The Tribal Council for The Oglala Lakota Sioux on The Pine Ridge Indian Reservation. He is famous (infamous?) for his involvement with the American Indian Movement (AIM).

He was a young man living on the reservation when he met Vernon Bellacourt, Russel Means, Dennis Banks, and John Trudell at an Indian rights protest in Minnesota. After that, he quickly and passionately embraced becoming one of the original members of the American Indian Movement, better known as AIM.

AIM is a group…more of a *family* of brave modern-day warriors for Indian rights. They began as a grass roots movement out of Minnesota in July of 1968 as a result of racism and the violation of Indian rights. It wasn't bad enough that we were taking all the land away, oh no. We had to horribly mistreat them as well and chip away at their very souls…their dignity. Well, in 1968, there were some young Indian men who weren't tolerating it any longer. These courageous souls got together and began to *demand* their civil rights. I was only eleven years old when most of the trouble started on the ridge, but I became obsessed with reading and learning about it.

Upon meeting Tom as a young adult, I sat and listened closely as he told me stories about those days. It fascinated me that he actually *knew* Anna Mae Aquash, the amazing Indian woman who was murdered by the feds…the real-life story behind the movie *Thunderheart* starring Val Kilmer and Sam Shepherd. In real life, that woman was a pillar of strength to so many and a hero to me. She fought for the rights of her people, protesting water poisoning, mining, racism and much more.

They actually filmed *Thunderheart* on Pine Ridge and my "niece," Evangeline Poor Bear, was in the scene when the home of "Maggie," who was the character based on Anna Mae Aquash, was buffeted with bullets, injuring a child that Val Kilmer rushes to the hospital. Wikipedia likes to call the movie a "fictional portrayal loosely based on real events"; however, Wiki is *wrong*. The movie is an attempt to tell the true story. Unfortunately, those who were trying to do so were forced to change names and juxtapose situations in order to get it out of the can. Make no mistake, the *true* story is far more complex and horrifying than the events of the movie *Thunderheart*. Robert Redford courageously produced and narrated a film entitled *Incident at Oglala* that lays it all out. The sickening truth behind everything. If you haven't seen it, I highly recommend you do so. Robert Redford is an extremely talented director and is known as a fearless champion for Indigenous Rights throughout the country. He brilliantly tells the true story of what went down. Be prepared to be astonished.

In the late 1960s, there was an incredible amount of violence occurring on Pine Ridge. The president of the tribe at the time was Dick Wilson, a puppet installed by the BIA to run the tribe "their way." Dick Wilson abused his power and took advantage of his position by terrorizing the good people of Pine Ridge with his "goon squad." There were so many uninvestigated deaths and incidents of violence that the American Indian Movement came to Pine Ridge to investigate and exercise their right to protest. The people of the tribe had unsuccessfully tried to impeach Wilson and end the conflict between the Wilson goon squad and the "fundamentalist/traditionalist" (AIM supporting) population; however, the BIA and FBI were intermingled within their corruption. The feds had given what they thought to be the most useless land to the indigenous, only to find out later that valuable oil and minerals were there in abundance. They found a much sought-after mineral, zeolite, in the badlands, along with many dinosaur bones and the national parks (the feds) were desperately trying to mine and excavate in sacred areas that hadn't even been *walked on* in hundreds of years. In 2003 they attempted to strip mine a particularly sacred area of the badlands at the southern edge called "The Stronghold." It was named that because that is where the Lakota women and children ran to hide during the massacre at Wounded Knee in 1890. The Ghost Dancers would perform on a ridge above a deep vertical valley. Genocidal murderers would shoot them as they danced against the moonlight, their bodies falling and landing in the valley which became known as "The Sacred Basin" and closed to most people.

In 2003 I went to the reservation to help with protesting against the National Parks Service who were attempting to excavate that very same area. In order to be granted a moratorium to stop the dig, the Lakota were *forced* to show photographs of the bones and other evidence that it was the final resting place for Native Americans, thus deemed "sacred land." I was there just to make and hand out peanut butter and jelly sandwiches to the gatherers when Tony Two-Bulls' truck (the only truck able to make it down the vertical approach to the valley), tumbled over itself, and they needed another appropriate vehicle. John Yellow Bird Steele, the THEN president of the tribe, spied the vehicles in the parking area and shouted, "Whose Excursion is that?"

I heard several people answer, "Skye's! That's Skye's new Excursion!"

At the tented food table, I cringed. I knew it was coming, so I waited for him to approach me.

"John, I can't! NO! Dan just *bought* this thing; he will *kill* me if anything happens to it!"

He looked at me with genuine empathy and explained to me that it was their only chance to get down there.

"There are no other vehicles that can pull it off, Skye," he said. Adding, "If we break it, I will replace it."

Before I knew it, I was smashed in the front seat with George Tall driving, at least thirty people in the back for weight, about ten of us in the front and middle seats. I will never forget it, my hands on the windshield as we slowly, 100 percent vertically, descended the cliff. Everyone in the truck was singing a prayer in Lakota, and I was *begging* George to take good care of the truck. George *and* the truck both did a great job, and we made it down to the sacred basin, where no humans have been in over two hundred years. The atmosphere down there was…*thick*, almost oppressive. It felt as if we were on another planet. I looked around in awe and disbelief. There were skulls of animals from long ago half buried in the dirt. I had a strong creepy feeling of being watched. The energy was palpable. It is and always will be one of the most incredible experiences of my life.

Two years prior to that, in 2001, I had gone on the first "Crazy Horse Ride" since becoming sick. This is an endurance horse ride of nearly one hundred miles in five days. This ride is organized by Bamm and his family. It started out a handful of riders, but after several years became almost two hundred participants who rode out of Fort Robinson, Nebraska in honor of Crazy Horse. Thasunke Witko, the great warrior Crazy Horse, who never had the chance to ride out, for he was murdered there. I was forced to skip the ride for 1999 and 2000, so I pushed myself to go in 2001. Completing the ride that year was one of the toughest accomplishments I have ever achieved. The pain was nearly impossible to bear, and I was still sore and recovering when, back at home, Dan and I celebrated his birthday on September 10th. The next morning, we watched in horror as the airplanes flew into the twin towers. The whole thing was so disturbing and upsetting that it completely distracted me from my constant pain and exhaustion. I marveled yet *again* at the evil in this world and counted my blessings. Dan has relatives on Manhattan, and we were unable to enquire about them for days. Thank God, when we were able to... they were safe.

Back in 1999, once I had dropped off Demi to the airport and Peggy at her house, I pulled into the driveway upon the conclusion of our road-trip, throwing the van into park. I was so exhausted that I could have literally closed my eyes right then and there and fallen asleep. I felt so weak. Dan and I pulled all my stuff out of the vehicle; it took every ounce of strength I had to check on the kids and my dad, giving them their souvenirs along with big hugs and kisses. Everybody wanted to hear all about the trip; however, I didn't have it in me, so I went straight to my bed. I told everyone that I was just *really* tired and needed to get some sleep. Maxx, who had been vying for my attention since I walked in, was more than happy to jump into bed to snuggle with me. He kept making this weird whining sound as we laid there. At the time, I figured he just really missed me, but looking back I think he was sensing that I was sick. His cold nose probed me even more than usual.

I had driven somewhere in the neighborhood of sixty hours, so I attributed my fatigue to that. It is so strange to remember telling everyone that evening that I was "Okay! Just fine! I'm only exhausted!" before I hit the sack, because the next thing that I remember is waking up at 2:00 A.M. as if someone were stabbing me in the side with a hunting knife! I was literally screaming in pain...yelling at Dan, "Ohhh oow! I am not okay...So *NOT* okay! What the fuck?!"

Thankfully, Dan is good in a crisis. He threw some clothes on and scooped me up to carry me to the car, because I couldn't move. I was rolled up into the tightest ball I could *be* in, holding my right side, and there was no way I was walking anywhere. All I could do is scream, and I was doing one hell of a job at that.

Although the pain was on the right side, I knew it wasn't my appendix, because mine had been removed years ago. Besides, this pain was more on my side…a flank pain, not an abdominal pain, and a totally different feeling. When my appendix had burst, I had a deep throbbing broad pain. This pain was literally stabbing me like a knife!

Poor Dan. He was so freaked out…we both were. He sped to the hospital, and I screamed out the window. I suppose, now that I think about it, you may have thought we were in labor had you caught sight of us en route.

I kept staring at my body, expecting to *see* what was causing all the pain, but there was nothing to see. I found it hard to believe that it was really happening.

I don't remember much of the next few days. They are a blur… a montage of pain, humiliation, nurses faces, family, flowers…an endless stream of doctors, one after another and Dan…Dan was a constant. I didn't communicate with anyone *except* him for days. I kept falling asleep and waking up, and I didn't have the energy to even ask questions. I was silent. Dan fed me my meals and cared for me with such love and respect that I couldn't put it into words if I tried.

Then, one day, I woke up and felt extremely lucid. I took a moment, because it had been a while, but I caught myself up. I had many questions, and Dan lay sleeping on the couch in my room. I was trying to wake him up. My voice was hoarse from not speaking for days, and my eyes were swollen as if I had been in a boxing match. Since I wasn't succeeding verbally, I started throwing things at him as he slept on. I chucked a box of Kleenex, then an empty IV bag that was within reach. I was *just* about to go for the pitcher of water when suddenly a doctor strolled in and looked down on me asking, "How are we doing today?"

I gave him an incredulous look, hoarsely and sarcastically told him, "Well, let's see; YOU are on both feet and smelling fresh like Old Spice… I am half dead lying flat on my back, and I can no longer tolerate the smell of myself… you do the math."

Ignoring my cynicism, he continued. "It is good to see you awake," he said, warming up his stethoscope.

I didn't answer this time; I was wondering just what he intended to do with that stethoscope.

Meanwhile, Dan had risen and was tucking in his shirt, staring at me in shock. He came to my bedside and kissed me on the forehead, which was the only place he *could* kiss me due to tubes, oxygen devices, and IVs. I looked at him strangely, and then back at the doctor.

"I need to know what is going on," I told him, attempting to sit up. I could hardly *believe* how listless I felt.

The doctor pulled up a chair and sat next to my bed. He had a concerned look on his face, and I saw him take a deep breath…

Oh great, I thought…*Here we go…*

"Just lay back and try to relax" he told me. "I'm going to try to explain to you what's happening. It's complicated, but you seem like an intelligent woman. I think it's imperative that we get a treatment plan started in order to address any questions and concerns you may have, so we must discuss everything."

I gave up on trying to sit up and laid my head back down however, I was nowhere *near* relaxed. I could see sympathy in his eyes, and I was scared to death to hear what was coming…

"You are very ill," he began.

The rest of what he told me goes as follows. I do not remember the words verbatim, but *this* is what I learned that dreadful day. The doctor told me…

"You have a very rare infection aggressively killing you. Four days ago, we knew that you were dying, but we didn't know *why*. We discovered that your right kidney suffered an embolism although, again, we didn't know *why*. Yesterday, I was lucky enough to catch the murmur as I carefully listened to your heart. It is very faint, but it's there. I am now convinced that you have a blood infection that has settled on a heart valve, so I drew blood cultures. Streptococcus is already growing strong. We are having a difficult time isolating the strain, but we are making progress. What we are looking for is that perfect cocktail of antibiotics to kill it. Knowing the strain will help greatly. We are doing all we can. If we are able to get rid of the infection, you will probably need heart surgery…"

If…? Did he just say IF?

"…we won't know until we run a few cardiac tests, but if I am right, there was *so* much infection on your heart that your valve threw an embolism…a clot of vegetation that hit your right kidney causing it to infarct… have a stroke. That is why you had all of that stabbing pain in your flank. I may be getting ahead of myself here… you will be going through many tests to confirm all of what I am saying, but the most important thing right now is to get rid of the infection, because it is killing you. It is also important to consult

with cardiology in an effort to minimize the damage to your heart muscle before cardiomyopathy sets in, because *then* we will be talking about a heart *trans-*
plant as opposed to a mitral valve repair."

I was frozen and terrified as he went on…

"Now, we have been trying some of the toughest antibiotics known to man
on you to no avail. Researching, I found a case that was able to kill this infection using both penicillin and gentamycin twenty-four hours a day, seven days
a week, for five weeks. So, at this time, you have two antibiotics going at once.
I am quite confident that this is going to work. It is already showing signs that
it will. Your vitals are much better! You scared us there for a while! I have been
doing this for a long time, and I have never before seen a blood pressure get
that low without losing the patient! Don't worry though, we have it up now,
and I am comfortable with letting you go through certain tests today and tomorrow so that we can get a treatment plan going. We have a cardiologist
coming in to see you today…soon, actually, so I am glad you are awake. He
will order tests that will tell us more about what's going on with your heart. It
will most likely take more than a month to get rid of the infection, and you
certainly can*not* have the heart surgery until the infection is gone. There are
decisions that you need to make and options to discuss with your heart surgeon. Do you have a cardiologist?

I managed to shake my head "no".

"You do not have to go with our consult. I mean, it's no *secret* that Loyola
is *the* place to go for the heart. We will begin with our cardiologist while you
research things. Now, any questions?"

Any questions? Is he serious?

Listening to the information from Doctor Kitaka, a nephrologist who had
clearly saved my life… left me speechless. I just stared at him with panic behind
my bulging eyes. I shook my head "no" again. After an odd stare, he continued,
"I am certain that you will have *many* questions once you process what I've
just said and after your consult with cardiology. Write them down….your questions. During times like this, it is easy to forget. Try not to worry."

Yeah, right…who's worried?

Abruptly, I attempted to dash for the bathroom only to crumble from
noodle-leg syndrome and be yanked back by my IV and other tubing. Doctor

Kittaka sprang into action to assist me just in time for me to vomit all over him. I must give him credit for playing it off so well…you'd have thought that I spilled a little apple juice on him. Grateful… I tried harder to hold my vomit down while he untangled my IV so that, with Dan's help, I could reach the toilet and finish. The heaving was violent. The contents of what was coming up was pure yellow slime.

The good doctor wasn't hanging around for any more of the barf-o-rama, he was *out of there* as quickly as possible. My nurse had since come into the room, and as she cleaned me up, I realized I was crying. My head throbbed as I clumsily made it back to my bed. The nurse promised to return with medication. And I attempted to do as the doctor suggested and tried to process what was just said to me.

Dan and I stared at each other in shock, neither knowing what to say. He tried to ease my concern by saying, "Okay…so we have a few things to clear up before you get back to our life."

No problem, I thought…I got this! Maybe I won't even *need* the heart surgery!

As if on cue, the cardiologist came in to give me my consult, and afterwards I felt much better. He told me there is "no emergency for the heart surgery; we need to get rid of this infection. As far as the heart valve is concerned, we need to keep an eye on it, that's all."

A feeling of relief washed over me as I put two and two together. If the heart was *that* bad, no decent cardiologist would say the things he said the way he said them. Little did I know *then* that "decent" would be the operative word of this thought *and* the reason I couldn't, putting two and two together… come up with four.

I decided to try to sleep, but I just *couldn't* get comfortable. My nurse returned with Demerol and versed for my IV, and finally, mercifully, I knocked off.

Although it had been many years since I had seen him, I *did* know another cardiologist…an excellent one actually, quite well. He didn't practice at this hospital; however, I learned to trust him as he cared for my dying mother four to five years ago. At the onset of her illness, we were butting heads…yet we took to each other eventually and actually became friends.

When I was *finally* released from the first hospital I was in, I had an appointment set with the cardiologist who evaluated me there; however, I wanted to see Dr. John Bajgrowvich, the doctor who cared so wonderfully for my mother. I figured surely a second opinion is a good idea in such a case, now that I was wishing I had pursued a second opinion for the hysterectomy. Only a fool wouldn't learn this from what I had been going through. I made an appointment with his office and tried to get accustomed to my "new normal" which was about as *abnormal* as it could possibly be.

I was released from the hospital with what is called a Groshong PICC line. It's a 24/7 IV that runs off a small battery system contained in what looks to be a "fanny-pack" but hangs from a shoulder strap as opposed to being carried around your waist. Let me tell you, that was *SOME FUN* when they put that in! They slowly fed plastic tubing through my superior vena cava (the large vein in my arm) with no local and not much warning. I writhed and screamed, suffering in agony while the nurse looked at me with sympathy as she maneuvered the tube up my vein. It was not unsimilar to feeding a drawstring through the string holes of a "hoodie" sweatshirt… only **REALLY PAINFUL**. The first chance I got, I jumped off my bed and hid behind it like a child who doesn't want a shot. They assured me that the "pop procedure" was almost over, as they tried to coax me out from the corner. Glancing down, I was a little freaked out at seeing a tube protruding from my vein, so I slowly came out from my stronghold. Quickly, they bent the tubing to stop it from bleeding as if they would bend a garden hose to keep it from spraying.

My emotions were all over the place; I was excited to be going home, angry from all of the medical man handling, and genuinely scared to death of what was to come. I remember one of the nurses telling me, just before my little escape, that if I didn't have the PICC line inserted I would not be able to go home. It took a bit to register…I was already behind the bed, but because of *that* I settled down. I had been in the hospital for a month…but it felt like a year, asking each morning if I could go home. By the time a month went by I was no longer *asking*…I was losing my *shit* like Jack Nicholson in "The Shining."

Upon leaving, I was told that a home health nurse would visit me at my house and check the unit and myself out to make sure I was caring for everything properly; however, no one ever showed up. I did my best with Dan's help;

unfortunately, that vein in my arm blew up like a giant purple balloon two days later and felt as if it were going to explode. Panicking, we rushed right back to the same hospital I was fighting for an entire month to get out of.

This was only the second time I found myself in the ER; the first time being when I had the stabbing pain from the kidney infarct at the beginning of this current nightmare.

Upon arriving there, I was mortified to find that since my first visit there were mandates recently put into place regarding my medical treatment. Now, since being diagnosed as "ambulatory yet critical" with the heart condition, I was no longer to be given an average butterfly needle for an IV...oh no. *Now* I was to have the *ginormous* 5 pt. HEP needle that *barely* fit in my vein! It felt as if they were attempting to nail my arm to the bed! I thought someone was going to put their foot on my forehead there for a minute to keep me still. There were four of them around me and room for no more as I screamed in anguish. I remember thinking,

This is as bad as that PICC line!

After the chaos finally slowed to an anxiety-ridden lull, they adjusted the PICC line (fun stuff) so that it performed properly. Once the "mob in white" was done groping me to be assured that my heart wasn't in active failure, I was allowed to go home. Now, I'm not personally familiar with how it feels to be gang-banged, but I bet it's close to what I had just experienced! I cried the entire way home...Dan was uncharacteristically quiet. We were both a bit traumatized. I guess it had to be difficult for him to watch, stifling the desire to help me fight them off.

On the car ride back, I was a miserable bitch from hell. I was crying and ripping angrily into Dan all at the same time. Looking back, I don't know *HOW* he tolerated me. I would have left *myself* on the side of the road! His patience with me still astounds me to this very day. I was a mess and *so* bad that I actually got on my *own* nerves. A good example would be when we arrived home that day from the ER. Dan walked around to my side of the car to help me get out, and I opened the door slightly then kicked it hard, ramming it smack dab into his torso! On top of THAT, I *hurt* myself *doing* it and collapsed pathetically into his arms crying...seeking his sympathy. He just held me. He comforted me. How the hell did he *DO* that? I don't think I could do that with another adult human! Maybe my dad, an animal, or a child, but not a grown-ass person. Is that an awful thing to say? It's the truth. From day one, that man cared for me as I would have only cared for a parent or one of the children I'd given birth to, under the same circumstances. His patience is ordinarily quite thin with others. As a boss, he is a tough task master and sets the bar high for his employees. To himself, he is even *worse*! Along with being a work-a-holic, he is a perfectionist. This man micromanages a dynamic business and deals with stress on an unfathomable level, yet with *me* he smiles, listens, tolerates, and understands.

Ironically, I had noticed myself getting annoyed and short with others months before becoming sick. Not quite sure *why*, I had prayed for patience. I suppose it was like a *lesson* in patience that I was given instead. I was thrown into a medical nightmare while trying to help care for my father, my children, and our business. Ummm….Thank you?

There is that saying that healthy people like to quote…

"God only gives us as much as He thinks we can handle."

Well, if that is true, then God must think I'm a *badass*, because…well, you will see. We are only getting started.

The first day I was out of the hospital, I made an appointment with Dr. Bajgrowich from Gottlieb Hospital. This was too important NOT to get a second opinion, and I trusted this man.

Sitting in his waiting room, I couldn't stop thinking of my mother…we called her Mumu, which is Finish for Grandma. She was who I always wanted to be…who I aspired to be. My mother was selfless, kind, intelligent, and loyal to a fault. A mother like no other. I missed her terribly and was still mourning her like she had died yesterday. In 1999 my mom would have been gone only four years, and I am not very good at losing those I love. My oldest brother Bobby had been gone for six years at the time, and I *still* had difficulty talking about it. I had issues with death my entire life, and I figured I always would.

I tried to lighten up a little in the waiting room. I thought about the day that Dr. Baggs and I were meeting in the hospital cafeteria to discuss my mother's test results, and I tried not to smile at the irony of being here as his patient. An amusing exchange between he and myself kept coming to mind. Four years earlier, Dr. Bajgrowicz had asked me to meet him in the cafeteria of the hospital for lunch, so we could talk about my mother's condition, discuss differentials, ask and answer questions and such. Evidently, he preferred it to me stalking him throughout the entire hospital in order to talk to him. Although I didn't *mean* to be, my sisters and I were a force to be reckoned with when my mom became sick. "Dr. Baggs," as we endearingly referred to him, never knew what hit him when the Gattone women descended upon him, the poor guy. My siblings and I had an inordinately close relationship with my mom. When she became ill, we literally freaked out. I spent many nights sleeping in the waiting rooms, as not to miss any doctors who came to see her. My mother was never alone. The family took shifts; however, I stayed even when it wasn't my turn. At this point in my life, I had never been more afraid.

After finding each other in the hospital cafeteria, our plan (Dr. Baggs and I) was to get our food and meet by the dining area.

I remember…

The cafeteria smelled like simmering, unfulfilled dreams and soup. Employees passed each other…their little hair net hats in place, oblivious to any and everything other than what was currently in their hands or in front of their faces. They narrowly avoided each other as they passed, going about what must have been second nature tasks. I looked up to check out the menu on the wall. So many things were going on in my head that I couldn't think clearly. I noticed a short layer of dust covering the *allegedly* clean plates as I grabbed one and wiped it off with the tail of my shirt. For some unknown reason, I was nervous.

"Well?" asked the man behind the counter as he quickly went from looking at me to staring right past me as I lifted my head.

"Umm," I answered him, or I thought I did.

"What will it be?" he said, this time much more assertively.

Now, he was looking directly at me again… aggravated that I couldn't read his mind. Nervously, I answered, "Grilled cheese?" It came out as a question.

"You're eatin' it," he mumbled under his breath as he dramatically dropped one on my extended plate. I noticed I was …*shaking*. Looking annoyed, he asked me, "Fries?"

"Um, sure," I answered him, as if he were the soup Nazi, and I feared losing my lunch.

Why was I shaking? Too much coffee this morning…

I grabbed a Pepsi, paid for my tray, and scanned the crowded dining area. Once I found Dr. Bajgrowicz, I made my way to the table and set down my tray. We both looked at the other's choices on our respective plates. The good doctor had a fish filet, rice, and veggies…I had my grilled cheese, fries, and a Pepsi. I searched the table for salt; finding none, I made the comment, "I'm going for salt, be right back."

Incredulous, he asked, "You're going to put *salt* on that garbage too??"

With a smile on my face, I reminded him that I was not his patient.

His expression wasn't exactly a returned smile as he answered, "Not *YET* you're not! Keep eating like *that* and it won't be long!"

We shared a laugh and lightened up a bit toward each other.

Sitting here in his office now, I thought of the irony of it all and about how everything seems to come full circle.

My name was announced by the nurse standing in front of an open door, and I was thrown back into the present. I followed her to an examination room. I remembered this nurse from years before. She obligatorily asked about my mom who I in turn told her had passed away.

"I am so sorry!" I could tell she felt bad.

I explained, "She had another heart attack while in Vegas and passed there." I added, "We were all by her side."

Deftly she gathered things as she told me, "We really loved your mom; again, I'm sorry." A soft, barely audible "Thank you" was all I could manage.

She put the pile that she had gathered on the examination table, explaining to me how I was to be ready for the doctor.

"Gown open in front; you can leave your panties on, but everything else needs to come off…open the door when you are done, and Doctor will be in."

The exam room immediately reminded me of my mother. I sat on the crunchy tissue-covered table, holding the gown and sheet and just cried. There was a soft rap on the door, and I quietly said, "Come in."

In walked Dr. Baggs with a worried look upon his face.

"Anna?" he asked. I nodded, and he walked straight over to comfort me. He hugged me, telling me, "It's going to be alright" and "Maybe it isn't so bad."

I interrupted him to explain, "Yes…it *is* that bad."

I told him that I was scared to death, but the tears were from thinking of my mom. He looked at me with genuine empathy, and in that very moment… I thoroughly comprehended his depth as a healer. I realized why I thought so highly of this man. I could tell he felt as if he *failed* or something. Whatever is happening to me, I remember thinking…

No one else is *touching my heart except Dr. Bajgrowvicz*…yes, his surname *is* just as hard to pronounce as it looks to be, *which is why my family and I refer to him as "Dr. Baggs". Ba-grow-vich is the phonetic pronunciation*….

Calling him "Dr. Baggs" is easiest.

Anyways…I had brought a copy of everything in my possession regarding the prior cardiologist.

Now, Dr. Baggs is a *doctor's* doctor. Throughout the years that he cared for my mother, I learned that he is a healer, a lifesaver…not just a doctor. He isn't some arrogant ego tripper on a power high. The very first time I saw the man, he was on a gurney that was being rushed through the halls of the E.R., straddling my mother's lifeless body performing CPR. He was coaching to her softly as he worked.

"C'mon now, *beat*, damnit…beat!"

It was, initially, very disturbing to see him pounce on her and watch him pound on her chest, but as I ran alongside the gurney, I could see that he was literally bringing her back to life before my very eyes.

I learned the difference between regular doctors and *real* doctors when I cared for my mother. There are doctors who adhere to the status quo, thus perpetuating the paradigm of low standards of care, and then there are the *real* doctors like Dr. Baggs. He thought outside of the box and considered every possibility. He cared deeply and *listened* to his patients. He once told me that he listens very closely, because "most people know their own body better than anyone else! Often, they hold the key to their own health unknowingly."

He also said that there were times when one of his patients would say or do something…even the slightest thing, that would result in him figuring out a complex issue about their condition. *That* impressed me. Dr. Baggs was there because he wanted to help people, not just for the money. I find that to be the difference between "healers" and most doctors. He is a healer.

There was one time, while my mother lay in a coma, I walked into her room and found him standing over her…just watching her sleep. We got started talking about her condition, and he told me of an idea that might work for a certain treatment that we had been worried to run and explained that he figured it out as he was standing over her just now. I remember thinking,

How many doctors do that?

I know the television doctors do it, but in real life... this is an endangered species. I had to word whip plenty of doctors who tried to treat me like an idiot regarding my mother. The only doctor who would speak to me eventually, without security present, was Dr. Baggs... and I was fine with that.

There were so many times when my sisters and I would inadvertently cause drama at the hospital while dealing with our mom's illness/death. Okay, fine. My oldest sister Mikki was pretty chill with them, but Kim and I were *beasts!* We would systematically search the entire hospital for either Dr. Baggs or his partner Dr. Ivfkovich, another fun name to try to say. We would walk in and out of patient rooms and even rap on the window of the door of the cath lab! Looking back, I am ashamed of my behavior; however, at the time I was ruthless; we all were...we were scared to death. Mom was our *everything!* She kept everything together. Mom was strong, sharp, and kept us all from *killing each other*...no way could she die! *Everything* had to be done, and it needed to be the *best* of everything, or my sisters and I would lose our *shit*, reducing the nurses (sometimes doctors) to tears with our razor-sharp tongues and wicked tempers.

They got in their fair share of punches...

One day I "caught" my mother's nurse washing her roughly while she was still in the coma, dropping her arm and tugging at her with what I thought to be less-than-gentle efficiency, and I kind of lost it. After chewing her ass out, I got permission to stay the night in the Cardiac Critical Care Unit...in my mother's actual *room* so that I could keep an eye on her and clean her myself. This was very soon after the initial incident, and everybody was still trying to be nice to each other. When Dr. Ifvkovich told the nurse that I would be staying, she left the room in a huff. Later that night, she came in and had a pill and a cup of water on a tray. I was aghast and said, "My mother is on a *respirator! She can't take a PILL!*"

The nurse was unfazed. When I was done speaking, she assertively explained, "This pill is for *you!*"

I tilted my head in confusion. She walked closer to me and said, "If *you* are spending the night, and I am pulling a double, then *you* are taking a va-lium!" She handed me the pill while looking around her for stealth purposes. "C'mon…bottoms up," she hurried me.

I took the pill before she changed her mind. I must admit, in spite of my-self…I was starting to almost *like* her at this point. I figure I *must* have been a nightmare for them! I found out later that they had cute little "pet" names for me. One was "ramrod" which, to their dismay, I found to be hilarious! The other ones…well, not so much. I can still remember turning the hospital cor-ridor corner to my mom's floor, seeing a known nurse walking straight towards me, then watching her abruptly turn around and head the complete other way. No wonder the kids call taking a U-turn "flippin' a bitch." Several times I had questions and/or concerns that they deftly ditched. I remember thinking,

Spineless sissies!

I now realize that they were merely avoiding a difficult, spastic family member of a patient in their care.

Although the internet existed, it was yet to become a trusted source to research my mom's condition…this was 1993-1994. I felt lucky to be living in Chicago though, where Northwestern Medical School and Library are located. Growing up, I clearly remember mom always saying how we were very fortunate to be surrounded by the finest medical schools and hospitals. I often thought about this little factoid of hers as I went from one hospital to the other and then another during *my* medical nightmare… usually rolling my eyes when I did. In my opinion, Chicago is to hospitals what Las Vegas is to casinos…they're everywhere; they are all similar; and it all boils down to luck.

Do you know how everyone always says, "Everything happens for a reason"?

Well, if that is true, I suppose the years of coping with my mother's ill-ness and eventual death had somewhat prepared me for what I was to endure four to five years later. I had come to know an excellent cardiologist whom I could trust.

I thought about the last interaction I *had* with my mom. It was the last time I would see her until after her final heart attack, coma, and death. The details of that day are seared into my memory. It was 1995, and my mother was to board a plane to Vegas where my father would meet her at the gate upon her arrival. Due to circumstances beyond our control, none of us were able to join her for the flight. The whole family gathered at the gate at O'Hare, surrounding my wheelchair-bound mother. Since her first heart attack, she became childlike due to the amount of time it took to bring her back. She had lost an awful lot of oxygenated blood to the brain and was an entirely different person. We were all crying and trying to explain to her that we *wanted* to accompany her on the plane, but things being what they were, no one was able to do so. This was before 9/11 when you were still allowed to escort and meet people at their specific gate. Mom was devastated about the fact that no one was going with her. I decided to ask the stewardess if I could just walk her wheelchair onto the plane and get her settled, to calm her. Seeing our anguish, she surprisingly acquiesced. She allowed, just myself, to pre-board my mother. I can still remember pushing her wheelchair onto the empty plane. I wanted to seat her in the front "bulkhead" area, and as I walked onward, I noticed only one head on board as I peered past the opened first-class curtain. The man quickly dodged my glance and kind of *slid* low into his seat. Evidently, he did not want to be seen and I couldn't have cared less. My mom had asked, *again*, if I would be sitting next to her.

"No, Momma, I'm so sorry! Daddy is picking you up at the airport when you get there."

My mother began to panic and cry, I was crying and trying to get her things situated before being asked to leave. It was truly heartbreaking, my mother begging me to stay and both of us crying like babies. We were hugging, her in the seat and I leaning over from the aisle. I felt a tap on my shoulder and assumed it was the stewardess *shooing* me out. I turned to look and standing right there in front of me was JERRY LEWIS, one of my all-time favorite entertainers! I was shocked yet too heartbroken to get star struck and continued to cry, for some reason even harder, holding my mother's hand in mine. For unknown reasons, I found myself shaking my head up and down, smiling and crying simultaneously.

"*Oh, you're the funny guy,*" my mother blurted out, breaking the tension. We laughed, I through my tears. Mr. Lewis handed me a handkerchief as I just stood there crying and looking from him to my mom. He said, "Forgive me, but I couldn't help but overhear…" I interrupted him, thinking we were being too loud, but he shook his head and continued, "I would like to help if that's okay. I will have your mother upgraded to first class, next to me, and personally walk her out to your father when we land. Would that help?" My jaw dropped. With the help of the stewardess, we sat my mom past the curtain into a large, roomy seat in the first-class cabin.

She had stopped crying and was asking Mr. Lewis if he was, "that funny guy on TV."

He and I exchanged smiles. Tears were still falling from my eyes, yet I was incredibly relieved. I thanked and hugged the kind man and kissed my mom goodbye.

"Buh-bye, Anna!" she cheerfully exclaimed, obviously oblivious to the prior tearful drama. She and Jerry Louis were waving to me as I walked half-backwards to exit the plane. The entire experience was incredibly surreal, and I hadn't thought about it much since it had happened. I still have that handkerchief.

Now, back to 1999, upon leaving the office of Dr. Baggs, I went straight to the testing facility to undergo yet more of the same tests I had undergone at the first hospital. Dr. Baggs wanted them done *his* way, by *his* technicians. Trusting him explicitly, I diligently had them finished in two days.

The follow up visit regarding the results of these tests is a day I will never forget, try as I might. Waiting for him to enter, Dan and I were joking around, even laughing; although I cannot remember what was so funny; however, I will *never* forget the look on Dr. Bagg's face when he entered the room to speak to us. Apparently, the joking was over.

He reluctantly explained to me that my heart sac was quickly filling with blood due to the fact that my mitral valve was no longer able to operate correctly. The killer infection had ravaged it, and it needed to be replaced as soon as possible. The worry on his face terrified me. He continued to explain what my imminent heart surgery would entail. I remember the feeling of shrinking into my cut off shorts as he went on to say that my sternum would be sawed, my body placed on the heart and lung machine as my heart was removed to be put into a magnifying structure. My heart would need to be cut open in order to get to the valve properly, and the mitral valve would need to be completely replaced by either a pig valve or an artificial valve. I thought I was going to vomit. I could barely wrap my mind around it…I was shaking my head "no" as he spoke.

Please, God, no.

I tried to fight his words. I told him that the cardiologist at the first hospital said it wasn't so bad and that they just "needed to keep an eye on it," and I watched as his face contorted.

"What?! What *doctor* told you this?!"

He was stupefied. He ranted that he couldn't *believe* an actual cardiologist would tell me this. We were all perplexed. I explicitly trusted Dr. Baggs and decided to stay as far away from the other doctor as possible. The other cardiologist had played *down* my medical situation...I just didn't understand *why* at the time. Later it would be revealed to me that Dr. Mengala, the hysterectomy menace, was in the same hospital, the same *group of practitioners*, as this so-called cardiologist...but that was to grace my comprehension much later... at trial.

Dr. Baggs recommended a specific surgeon for my heart surgery. I tried to tell him that I wanted *him* to do the surgery; however, he explained that my condition was far too complicated and risky for him to perform. I suppose *now* he does them with his eyes closed as this was nearly twenty years ago, however at the time, he refused to do it. The surgeon he recommended was a famous heart surgeon who operated out of Loyola and The University of Chicago Hospitals...sometimes Northwestern if that was where the high-risk patient was. I remember Dr. Baggs explaining to me that whenever the president was in Chicago, Dr. Bakhos, this recommended surgeon, would be called upon to stay within a certain number of miles of him in case of an emergency. He also told me that there are people who wait *years* to have their respective surgeries, as he was in such high demand. I remember this specifically, because my husband Dan sort of freaked out when he said it.

"My wife is not waiting for *any* surgeon!" he said.

Dr. Baggs calmed Dan down by saying that as soon as he hears of my situation, he will perform the surgery exactly when it needed to be done. Now, Dr. Baggs *knew* me...Dr. Bakhos did not, so I was asked to come into his office for a meeting first. I foolishly thought that this "meeting" was for my benefit...to get to know the man who was going to put his hands all over my heart. Later, I learned that it was for the surgeon to interview *me* before deciding whether or not to *take* the job.

I cannot help but smile when I think of that meeting. I instantly fell in *love* with Dr. Bakhos. Immediately. He is a small man with amazing eyes and a warm smile. He explained in horrifying detail what would be done to me, almost exactly as Dr. Baggs had said, in an intelligent, sweet, and calming way. I think he got a kick out of Dan and I as we were so out of sorts. He told me that I would need to choose which valve I was to have replace my ravaged one. He explained that I could either go with a pig valve or an artificial one.

Did he just say PIG VALVE?

I must have been in shock or something, because I listened to his entire speech without vomiting or passing out. I was quiet and attentive, yet strangely disconnected.

Dr. Bakhos gave me an artificial valve to wear around my neck, like a necklace. This was done so that I could experience exactly what it was like to have it in place. He explained that I would *hear* it and *feel* it afterwards and that this "necklace" would show me how it would be to live with an artificial valve.

When I first placed it around my neck, I remember thinking…

Well, this isn't so bad…

However, by the time we drove the ten minutes home, I wanted to chuck it out the window! There was *no way* I would be able to deal with hearing that all the time…*feeling* it constantly ticking like a grandfather clock stuck in my heart! I would go completely insane. I freaked out when I thought the *pig valve* would be my only option. Pig valves need to be re-done every five to ten years. Upon my second appointment, I literally *BEGGED* Dr. Bakhos to find another option. I was in tears. He sweetly explained that if one presented itself to him, he would do just that. I didn't completely understand, but when I reported back to Dr. Baggs, his jaw dropped.

I remember thinking…

He is genuinely "star struck" over this surgeon.

Dr. Baggs then explained that, in very rare situations, an extremely talented surgeon can actually find a way *around* replacing the mitral valve. I was ecstatic! I *pleaded* with Dr. Bakhos every time I saw him, whining that he *must* find another way. His eyes would twinkle with a "Mona Lisa" smile on his face as I pleaded, encouraging me to believe he already had an idea. At the time, I failed to realize how miraculous all of this truly was. Looking back, though, I believe it's because I was focusing on the things I thought I could control. I felt so helpless. I made a concerted effort not to think about dying, but that was difficult…I didn't like the odds I was given for surviving my surgery. The thought of being a long shot… 25 –30 percent, was hanging over my head like an anvil, and *that* was about all I could handle at the time.

My body continued to fight the infection, and I became weaker as time went on. I went through a phase of cleaning closets and organizing my things, imagining others going through it upon my death. I also became obsessed with writing letters. Letters to my loved ones. I tried to be witty and as non-dramatic as possible, but there were certain things I needed them to know. My intention was not meant to be negative, merely *thorough*. I thought a lot about how to tell my two boys. I emphatically refused to allow anyone to say a *thing* to them, but my boys are smarter than that…they sensed it. One night out of nowhere, my eldest stopped me from leaving his room after tucking him in… he asked, "Mom? Are you gonna *die?*"

I closed my eyes for a second and took the deepest breath I could manage. I sat back down on his bed and tried to explain to him that I just didn't *know*. I told him if that was the case, I wanted him to be happy and grow to be a good man. I asked him to look after his brother and father, reminding him that *nothing* comes before family. I explained to him that I would always be with him in his heart. My Jesse, always tough as nails…cried silently as he listened closely. I lightened up the mood by telling him I would send him *signs* from the afterworld. I would make the lights flash or something. He laughed through his tears as he told me to levitate his brother and drop him on his head. Before I left his bed that night, I opened the drawer of his bedside table and pulled out one of his precious comic books. He looked at me quizzically as I told him, "Here. Take a few minutes to read your stuff."

Relieved to see his eyes light up and quickly get "into" his story, I glanced at his little brother who was passed out cold, smiled, and closed the door. I couldn't wait to get into bed. I remember how thoroughly exhausted I was as the infection raged on. There were times when I just couldn't breathe. I was perpetually nauseous with a permanent headache, and it seemed as though *everything* hurt.

The legal battle had already begun while I was still in the hospital for that first initial month. From out of *nowhere*, an attorney called my room, proudly announcing he was with Chicago's "biggest medical malpractice firm." He asked me if he could come by the hospital to visit me, to which I said, "Sure."

When I asked him how he even *knew* about the situation, he simply replied, "Oh, we have our eyes and ears everywhere."

That gave me the creeps.

The big unknown at this point was where had this horrible infection come from. It didn't matter *how* many doctors came in to see me, and trust me, there were MANY; each one *knew* that the infection must have been related to or caused *by* the hysterectomy. The mystery was how…and why. It had been documented that I spiked a fever of 103 degrees seven days after the surgery. Also documented were all of those ridiculous cauterizes, phone calls, questions, and notes from each interview with the nurse every time I had gone into Mengala's office post surgically. Mr. Big-shot Lawyer Guy wanted to start digging for the truth (and the money). He needed my permission to file for certain medical records and get started; of course, I acquiesced. I had heard of this firm and seen their attorneys on the news. He wasn't lying when he bragged of being the largest med-mal firm in Chicago.

The personal attorney that they assigned me was quite the character! Let's call him "Seth," okay? It isn't his *real* name, but let's just call him that anyway.

Seth was a tall gangly man of six feet, at least. He was well-dressed and wore glasses over his beady little eyes. He must have had some sinus condition, because he was constantly pulling at his nose with a handkerchief. There are two things that stick out to me when I think about Seth. The first was that he kept telling me, as I lay in my hospital bed, that I was "earning the big bucks." It always annoyed me when he said shit like that.

The second thing, and the reason I sought out an alternative law firm, was that after a meeting in early November, Seth asked me if I would give him some of my pain pills. My husband and I were aghast. We decided that evening that we'd had enough of Seth… the human equivalent to nails on a chalkboard.

We did some research and found an ethical, *normal* medical malpractice lawyer who was located in DuPage County and was familiar with the workings of things there.

I came to learn that DuPage County cases were an entirely different animal than Cook County ones. Yes, Seth's group was a huge deal in Chicago, yet they were accustomed to *Cook* County…not DuPage. Cook County was the city; DuPage County was in the suburbs and where everything had occurred. We learned that DuPage County jurors were inordinately conservative and notoriously stingy. After failing to get the venue changed to Cook, I dumped the big-shot lawyer guy and settled on a sharp, hungry pit-bull of an attorney named Gary Grasso. Gary used to *work* for a large insurance company until he switched teams and started defending people *from* them.

We figured that if anyone knew the way things worked there, it would be him. Upon some checking, I found that he maintained an impressive record and reputation. After meeting with many other DuPage County firms, I settled on Gary Grasso of Grasso Law which is, by the way, his actual name. So, let the games begin!

I found out the hard way that being the defendant in a high-profile medical malpractice case is the legal equivalent of what I was going through medically. Tortuous, beyond frustrating, and completely inhumane. There were endless meetings, interrogatories, professional photography shoots of scars, depositions, hearings, and even a private investigator following me *everywhere*. The trial wouldn't begin for a few years; however, the busy-work was constant and in full swing.

I remember when I saw the court room for the first time. I was intensely intimidated. Here I was, *finally* going to get my "day in court," and I almost peed myself. In my own defense, I had just been painstakingly put back together like Humpty Dumpty complete with a "hold her body together" metal medical girdle from *hell*! I suppose we should go *there* first, yes?

Okay, so I *finally* beat the infection. The entire time I battled it, I tried to prepare myself for the big surgery. Being confined to first, my bed at home and then the hospital, I had plenty of time to think. I *thought* that I had the time to get to all of the great books I hadn't time for before, and I tried! It's just that *everything* I read would remind me somehow of the predicament I was in and make me think of death. I would read for a few minutes, then I would cry or start a new list or letter. I am quite certain that I was losing my mind. I couldn't eat, couldn't sleep, couldn't read, and could only write short, dark poems and sappy "goodbye letters" to the ones I loved. I was in a state of self-pity stasis. The usual ubiquitous, opinionated Anna had been reduced to a "deer in the headlights" zombie. The only time I would perk up was when I got to see my kids. Dan would bring them often, and I would spend the entire morning "practicing" acting normal. Like I said before, my boys are wise bey-ond their years, and I now know that I was wasting my precious energy trying to convince them that I was going to be "just fine" and "getting better."

Prior to the heart surgery, I spent approximately three weeks as an in-pa-tient at Gottlieb due to my heart's precarious condition. My small body was fighting so hard to stay alive with the help of the nurses and Dr. Baggs. We became great friends, Dr. Baggs and I, throughout this time. I would wake to find him asleep in the visitor's chair. He was always straight up with me and he would diligently listen to my fearful rants and emphatically tell me "YOU ARE NOT GOING TO DIE!"

I foolishly made him promise me. I guess he figured either he would be right, or I would be gone anyways. Dan thinks he promised because he *knew* that Dr. Bakhos was THAT good.

One particularly crazy moment was when I was talking to Dr. Baggs, and suddenly I couldn't breathe at all. There was no air going in or out. My eyes were wide with terror, and the good doctor calmly leaned me back and com-pressed twice on my chest until I was breathing again. I still get the chills when I think of that time. My heart was failing at random times, but that was the only time I distinctly remember being lucid for it. It was pretty fucking scary. I remember him hollering, "Code! Coding in here!"

I can still see all the people rushing in with medical paraphernalia; it was so bizarre! When I took my first good breath, I remember feeling like I had been under water and had finally gotten to some air. I am so glad that Dan wasn't there for that. It would have scared the hell out of him.

Dan. He always stayed positive, kind, and gentle… methodically caring for me yet full of humor and compliments. I resembled the girl who comes out of the well of the movie *The Ring*, yet he would burst into my hospital room asking where his beautiful bride was. I know I must have been a night-mare to deal with…I am painfully aware of my personality type and that poor Dan was the whipping post. For that I will *always* be intensely grateful yet just as remorseful.

My medical captors were kind enough to allow me a couple of days with my family prior to the big surgery. I was advised "to get my affairs in order" just in case. A 26 percent chance wasn't really my type of bet to take, so I was pretty scared. I had already told Dan everything I wanted as far as a wake and burial. I told him *closed casket*, or I will *haunt* you for the rest of your life. He laughed and said, "Good…you will still be around then!" He got the *hairy eyeball* for that one.

I had written a letter to everyone, cleaned my messy drawers, and specified who was to get what as far as my jewelry and other treasures were concerned.

I decided to save the night before surgery just for Dan, the boys, and I but went on and planned an evening with my *whole* family two days before going in. I believe that day was the last day of November; the heart surgery was on the second of December. My sisters came over and made our traditional pasta dinner with the rest of my family and a few friends. Dan wanted to do something special like go to the Bahamas, but I told him, "No."

I explained to him that one of our "family movie nights" was what I wanted… nest and all. I *loved* our time with everybody *and* with just the four of us and wanted to do both.

Ever since the boys were very little, Dan and I would randomly deem a "family movie night." We would agree on a movie and put together a huge bed of layers of cozy blankets in front of the TV. We would lay there, the four of us…watching a movie together. We called the bed, our "nest." In our nest, there was laughter and love, tickling by Dan and bickering between the boys. There was popcorn everywhere! Maxx took care of most of the popcorn *and* took up the most room in the nest. The boys would use his long, soft body as a pillow. The kids could literally do *anything* to or with Maxx without him getting angry. He would just whine until I made them stop. They would put sunglasses on him, attach him to a skateboard to pull them…you know, crazy, stupid child ideas of fun. Maxx would have an anguished look on his face, but he wasn't fooling me…*he loved it.*

One night before all this craziness began. We were all curled up in our nest…our own little world. My heart felt squeezed as I looked at my peaceful loved ones and I thought…

It just doesn't get any better than this

For once, I was right. It never *did* get any better than that. Oh, how I *longed* for those hectic days and cherished nights of relaxation.

Looking back now, I think I was trying to recreate that very evening. It wasn't possible. That was the day I learned to revel in *every* moment of life. You cannot recreate them.

Ever since coming home, my large, beautiful German shepherd, Maxximus was a bit on edge. He was always right next to me, but now he wasn't even letting me go into the *bathroom* alone. He whined at confusing moments, dropping his huge paw into my lap. I must admit that it worried me to see how nervous *he* was.

Okay, so I was home from the hospital just for a couple days to spend with family and friends before the major heart surgery…

We tried to make everything as normal as usual; however, neither of the events were even *close* to average. There was sadness hanging in the air around us on both days. I had foolishly imagined an average family night, and I couldn't have been more naïve.

There were some good moments… some genuinely funny ones. Dan had donned an apron and helped with dinner, and we laughed at *and* with him. Of course, the kids had funny remarks and questions…my poor nephew Bobby was only eighteen at the time, and I had been a constant in his life from birth. I don't think he left my side for the entire get-together. He was so sweet; he asked me if there was "anything I wanted to tell him." I looked into his eyes and saw fear.

"Don't be scared, Bobby," I told him.

Then I took that opportunity to tell *everyone* that I had written them individual letters…just in case. You could have heard a pin drop after I said it, so I went on nervously, "Hopefully, you will never even see them."

The silence persisted, so I added, "Hey, let's *EAT!* I'm *starving.*"

Finally, everyone snapped out of it, and I took a deep breath…or at least I *tried* to. The closer I came to the heart surgery, the harder it was for me to get a decent breath. It was like I could breathe but not to the point that was satisfying. I could *feel* death coming for me. I must admit; I was convinced I would die. I tried to stay positive, but the way I *felt* made it close to impossible. I could *feel* the energy leaving my body…like a car running out of gas.

Everybody was pathetically trying to act normal, although none of us were pulling it off. Papa was the only one who came close to being "normal," and *he* was repeating himself over and over again.

He looked genuinely shocked every time the word "surgery" crept into the conversation and asked with a furrowed brow, "Who's having *surgery?*"

Each time I would say, "Me, I am Daddy."

He would look straight into my eyes and say, "Oh! Honey, I'm so sorry! Are you gonna be okay?"

I told him, "Yes, Daddy. I will be *fine*."

Every. Single. Time. No exaggerating; he said it about fifteen times that day. God bless him. It was torture to watch his decline.

He was always such a "man's man." The boss...our fearless leader. The Big Guy who made all the rules, or at least Mom let him *think* so. Now, he spent the entire day asking if he should take his shoes off or not. Non-stop. It was horrific to watch as his once sharp mind slowly betrayed him. Alzheimer's is an evil disease that *steals* a person little by little until they are gone. It is one of those diseases that is more difficult for the caregiver than the victim of it.

On the day of the pasta dinner, my friends and family were trying way too hard. All of them were full of profound words that created awkward moments... and evidently everyone lost their sense of *humor*, because I couldn't *joke* about anything without hearing the proverbial

GOD FORBID, ANNA.

Jesse had a *million* questions, and I danced around them the best I could. Thank God for Cole's comic relief, bless his ten-year-old soul; it would've been a disaster of epic proportions. I was almost *relieved* when the time came for everyone to leave, and we were putting my dad and the boys to bed. After tucking in my dad, I insisted on an early night, because I wanted the boys to go to school the next day. Reluctantly, I was allowing them to miss the day of the surgery, the next day...however, I was adamant about them not missing two days. I remember Jesse telling me, "I don't know *how* you expect me to concentrate."

I told him that I was compromising. They could miss the day *of* the surgery and that was it. I explained to him that then the weekend would come, so he will have three days off of school instead of two. At the family party, while we were discussing it, Cole made everyone laugh by asking, "Hey, how many days do we miss if you *die*?"

Thank *God* everybody laughed with me. I thought it was hilarious.

Our private movie night went better than the family dinner. I had established some normalcy by making dinner (with Dan's help) and doing homework with the boys. It was like a Friday for them. They didn't have to go to school the next day.

Now, none of this was cool with me; however, it didn't seem fair *not* to let them wait with the rest of the family in the hospital.

I gave up and allowed it. Their aunties, cousins, and even some of their friends would be there, giving me little choice. I attempted one last time to get them to go to school; however, Jesse fiercely announced that if his cousins could miss school and his whole family was going to be there, he wasn't going *anywhere* except that hospital and that was *that*. My little warrior-gene boy. Outnumbered in my opinion by…*everybody*, I reluctantly gave in.

The night of the dinner party, Dan went in their room with me to tuck them in afterwards, and we ended up staying in there for almost two hours answering their questions. More accurately, *Dan* answered the questions; it was all I could *do* not to burst into tears and keep that calm smile on my face. No way was I going to have them remember me any other way. Afterall, I was trying *so* hard to maintain normality. I almost lost it when Jesse made one of his last statements, "You just don't want us there in case you *die*."

I immediately looked at Cole who was already sound asleep. Dan took the bullet for me and sat on Jesse's bed. I started to approach as well when Dan looked at me and asked, "Hey, Mom, can we have a few minutes alone?"

Dan must have sensed that I would drop the ball. I nodded my head, kissed my boys, and went to leave the room. Before I made it out, I threw over my shoulder, "Dan, let him read some of his comics before he falls asleep."

Jesse managed a smile and told me, "Mom? You're the best Mom in the whole wide world. I love you."

I remember thinking…

Hold it together, Anna; you're almost done.

I managed to tell him thank you and that I loved him too…so much that it was ridiculous. He always smiled when I said it that way. Although I wanted to stay, I knew Dan was right, and I quietly shut the door, checked on Papa, and then hit the bed.

I was thoroughly exhausted and miserably uncomfortable. I couldn't get into a suitable position; I kept shifting around getting aggravated, so I decided to take a shower. I was in the bedroom at my vanity, brushing out my long hair when Dan entered. I said, "Wow, you just got out of the boys' room? Did Cole wake up? Did you give Jesse his comic book?" I was babbling nervously.

My husband approached me, drew me into his arms gently, and answered, "Yes, no, and yes. Now try to relax."

"I'm fine!" I lied.

We just stood there holding each other. I thought about how no matter what happens, I had a good life. Short but sweet. I had a few "dreams" as a kid, and I had definitely nailed one...

I had found true love. A love that only grew stronger as we lived our dream life out...until it turned into this nightmare.

Dan tried to get seriously mushy. He told me that I was the love of his life and always will be. Gently, I asked him, "Let's not go there, okay?"

I knew that I'd had enough for one evening, and I still had to get through movie night the next day.

After dinner and homework, the night before the surgery, Dan put on the movie, and we all cozied up in our nest. It was traditional for Dan and me to sneak off for privacy once the boys fell asleep, so I fought to keep my eyes open. This was one night we really needed to do so. What helped to keep me awake was that I was jumping in and out of the shower throughout the whole movie.

I had been ordered to take three separate showers using Hibiclens, a powerful antibacterial wash that was difficult to lather and left my skin feeling like I had just walked the Gobi Desert. I was still getting used to the absence of my PICC line, making unnecessary adjustments in the shower as if it were still attached to me. Three showers. One down, two to go.

When I entered the room, Dan had candles lit and the TV off. Some of my favorite songs were playing softly in the background. It was very romantic. Dan was laying on his side, smiling. I lied down next to him and got into my special position for our entanglement. He kept telling me to be careful; I was adamant that we fall asleep entangled in each other's arms that night. The way we used to. I also wanted sex, and I told him so. His answer was a long, slow, wet wonderful kiss. After, he looked strangely at me.

"You sure?" he asked gently.

There had been little sex throughout fighting the infection as I was never in the mood.

"I'm like 26 percent sure," I said with a wink.

Dan and I had a great marriage and were just as in love with each other as ever…even *more so*; however, prior to this medical madness, we used to fall asleep in a special way, entangled just right. Since the dominos began to fall; however, if I wasn't in the hospital, Dan would be nervous and awkward about sex due to that stupid PICC line. He would even get nervous cozying…snuggling.

"PICC line's gone," I reminded him.

"Go take your second shower, baby," he urged me, adding, "The third one you should take just before we leave in the morning. You didn't eat anything, did you? It's past midnight already. Did you take a Xanax, so you will be able to sleep?" to which I replied, "Yes, no, and yes," with a smile.

We stood there in each other's arms, and suddenly I wanted him physically more than I ever have before. Slowly, while staring into my eyes, he kissed me. The kiss was soft and sweet, becoming more intense as it evolved into a straight up make out session. It was as if we were fifteen years younger and had to part ways.

I met Dan when I was in college. I would come home to work on breaks and some weekends. We met on spring break of 1985, carrying on a long-distance relationship until we just couldn't handle it anymore. Making out with him here felt like one of those nights when I simply *had* to go back to Western and he couldn't go with me. We both pushed it to the limit, he with his boss and I with my teachers, dance coach (or director).

We made love that night as if it were our first and last time together, rediscovering each other's bodies, kisses lingering in places not visited in months. We kept direct eye contact with each other. The lovemaking was sweet, soft, and gentle, and when we were finished, I asked him if he would wash my back in the shower. He scooped me up as if I weighed *nothing* and carried me into the bathroom. We made love a second time in the shower, I can hardly *believe* I had the energy. It was amazing. Then Dan scrubbed the tub thoroughly and filled it.

"You should probably soak in a tub now," he said.

We both laughed, making jokes about the surgical staff saying, "She looks clean, but what is that *smell*?"

By the time we hit the bed, we didn't have much time to sleep before we needed to leave for the hospital. We knocked off like rocks for the few hours we had…completely intertwined.

My dream was odd. I was in a strange house looking *everywhere* for Dan and the boys. I was searching each unfamiliar room, stepping over large dominos that lay on the ground touching each other and forming a long snake like trail through the entire house. I *knew* somehow that I had to get to the end of the trail of fallen dominos to find them, but it just kept going. I began to call out for them, when suddenly, I woke up sweating, panicking from not finding them in my dream. Shaking it off, I looked at the clock, gently kissed Dan's forehead as he slept and snuck off for my final, shitty shower.

The morning was hectic. I had a difficult time leaving the house. I kept thinking…

"Am I going to come back?"

"Is this the last time I leave my house?!"

I was thoroughly annoyed that I couldn't have anything to eat or drink. I was thirstier than I had *ever* been, or so it seemed, and was *jonesing* for a cup of coffee as if it were crack cocaine and I a crack head.

Maxx was whining and "nosing" me all over; he was a wreck. I stayed next to him the whole time I was home, petting his worried face.

The kids were as animated as ever…maybe even more so. I have to smile when I think about that morning. I was quiet and reserved (scared to death), and those boys sensed it. They were so fucking cute! Jesse tormented Cole less than usual, stepping up to his big brother role. Cole, a bit nervous, kept trying to get me to talk…

"Mom. Mom. Mom…MOM… are you okay, Mom?"

"Yes, sweetheart, I am fine," I would answer him.

I remember his glare. Then he stole one of my own moves from my playbook.

"You sure? Look at me." He pointed his two fingers at his eyes.

I wish I had a dollar for every time I had done that to *them*.

In spite of everything, I smiled. He stood there waiting, so I stopped what I was doing, stared him straight in the eyes and lied…

"I'm *fine*, son…just fine!"

I felt terrible to lie to him, but what else was I to do? He kissed me and walked away. I almost missed what he mumbled under his breath.

"Liar, liar, pants on fire."

I laughed quietly as he walked away. Doing so eased my tension immensely; the cost being a sharp chest pain and a coughing fit.

After taking a few moments with Maxx, I started to tear up as I told him to "take good care of everybody if I don't make it back." Dan gently tugged me away, and we left.

I am glad we all drove to the hospital together, Dan, me, and the boys. It made it impossible for me to freak out. I had to be strong and positive. When we arrived, I went to check-in while Dan walked the boys over to the cardiac surgical waiting room. I almost crushed them while hugging them "goodbye".

I had tried to dissuade my family and friends from waiting the entire time while I was in surgery, to no avail. It was like a family get-together in that room.

I couldn't understand *why* they were all going to wait there for eight to eleven hours. Isn't that why we have telephones and shit?

The whole thing kind of creeped me out…all of them in there, like a wake.

I can still remember the patter between myself and the surgical staff that morning. Although I was scared to death, I used humor and levity to avoid dealing with my fear. I had developed this odd love/hate relationship with all things medical, so some of my jokes weren't exactly funny. I remember asking them if there was a pool going and was *anybody* betting on my survival. They were all very nice and assured me that I was in excellent care. Dan was allowed to be with me until I entered the OR. That's when it got sappy. He and I calling out I love You! I remember telling him to take good care of our boys. My tears were uncontrollable, I was shaking and beyond traumatized. The surgical team surrounded me and comforted me. Their kind faces and words were just starting to make me feel better when someone mentioned "fitting me for the chest saw." I remember thinking,

They couldn't name it something else.

The blood pressure device is called a sphygmomanometer for fuck's sake!

After a frightening mental image of my chest getting *sawed* open, I looked back at my anesthesiologist and asked to be knocked out. She kindly obliged. I felt a warm head rush and then peace.

At one of my pre-surgical appointments, Dr. Bakhos, my heart surgeon, had asked me if there was any particular music I would like played during the surgery. I told him, "Yes. The kind of music that makes YOU feel calm, confident and miraculous, Doc."

I recall that conversation quite clearly; however, I also recall that he never told me what that music would be.

Now I am fully aware of how crazy this sounds, and there's a huge possibility that the drugs were playing tricks on my mind, however, it is *so clear* and still so vivid to recall…

I was up on the ceiling in the corner of the operating room, way up high, watching my own surgery and listening to Bach. Someone was there with me; I just don't know who it was. It felt like my mom. I couldn't take my eyes off of the surgery. We watched, rapt. Dr. Bakhos's usual smiling face was concealed under a mask; I could tell he was all business. His big beautiful eyes were hidden behind a pair of odd glasses as he stared into my wide-open chest cavity.

The weirdest part of the whole thing was how I felt as I watched. I felt no sadness, no fear, no anxiety. I simply looked on, fascinated with what I was seeing. I also remember thinking or saying,

Oh, that poor thing. I hope she doesn't die.

I was thoroughly, emotionally detached from the body that lie before me. It wasn't *me*. I felt sympathy, but that was about it. Actually, empathy would be a better word. I felt sad for "her" even though it was my own body. Ever since that very *moment* I have known that we go on. I realize now that the body and the soul are completely independent of one another. We go on! Still to this day, as I sit here and type, Dear Reader, I don't *think* that we go on to another realm… I *KNOW* we do. After everything was said and done, after all the surgeries, the horrendous pain and injury, and the scars I was left with mentally and physically, *that* is what I was given spiritually. The *knowledge* that this physical life is *not* the end.

I have dreams sometimes of where I went; however, the memories are confusing. I know my mom was there. I also remember that there were colors "in that place" for lack of a better term, colors that we don't have here. I know how strange that sounds, but it's true. Everything there was in crystal clear high definition…so sharp, so distinct. The sky was incredibly beautiful and quite different from ours. The colors were mind-blowing! I wish I would have looked around more, but my attention was focused on the surgery. It was difficult to rip my eyes away from it.

After watching for a while, I just closed my eyes.

When I opened them next, I was in the throes of agony, being tormented by evil nurse number one and evil nurse number two. Among other things, they were deliberately denying me pain meds after having my chest sawed open. I writhed and cried until I finally fell off the gurney, coded (died), and was rushed back into the cardiac OR. They re-opened my chest in an attempt to revive me; however, they used the rib-spreader, and my bones were so brittle that they shattered. Typically, they do not like to use the rib spreader twice within twelve hours; however, they needed in order to bring me back to life. Several of my ribs snapped and my sternum splintered causing a post-surgical non-union. Dr. Bakhos reached into my re-opened chest and gently massaged my heart with his talented hands until it began to beat again. Talk about "heart hands!" Those were *genuine* heart hands.

Upon waking from the second heart surgery, I was in so much pain, that after a few questions, they put me into a medically induced coma.

I was placed in the CCU first, being a sketchy case. Blessedly, I had wonderful, normal, nurturing nurses caring for me this time, but the pain was ridiculous. It felt as though I had just been run over by a truck...a really big one.

I opened my eyes one day to find my bed surrounded by strangers in business clothing. Dr. Bakhos was among them, and he placed his hand on my arm and explained, "The other patients from the CCU reported everything that happened after the first surgery. I am so sorry, Anna."

There were mumbles from the others. None of them except Dr. Bakhos could meet my eyes as I looked around.

Okay, so I didn't dream the torture part...

He continued to tell me that both nurses have been fired, stripped of their licenses, and would *never* care for another patient. He asked me if I had anything to say to them. I thought about it for a minute and decided, yeah, I do. I nodded my head "Yes."

One of the "suits" left the semi-circle and returned with the two sadistic "nurses" who had tortured me. They both began to apologize at the same time. Again... as with the suits, neither was able to maintain eye contact with me as I stared at them. I let them babble a bit and then told them to "stop talking."

I stared at them, shaking my head, and finally, after not being able to come up with anything else, I said, "You disgust me."

I then looked at the host of suits and said, "Get them out of my sight."

Dr. Bakhos asked me if I wanted to file criminal charges and informed me that my lawyer was waiting to see me; however, he would like to speak to me first. I asked him, "What's with the group of rubberneckers?"

To which the doctor explained that they were employees of the hospital, lawyers, councilors, and such. I told him they could all go too. Each one approached me with obligatory apologies and a business card as they filed out. I noticed two suits remained. Dr. Bakhos explained that they were the hospital's lawyers, and they wanted me to sign a document stating that I wouldn't sue the hospital for what happened. I must admit; initially I was angry! I ranted about how evil those nurses were, and I asked if the poor drug addicts had to go through that same torture when they are in there and about how inhumane that is. Dr. Bakhos told me that my attorney was waiting to talk to me and that he didn't want me to sign *anything* before speaking to him. At that time, the ever annoying Seth was still my attorney and his messed-up nose smelled more money. I, however, had other things on my mind.

I was more concerned about the surgery, how it went and what kind of valve I ended up with. I learned that miraculously, Dr. Bakhos had repaired my ravaged mitral valve by removing part of my aortic valve and wrapping it around a plastic O-ring that would hold up my *own* natural mitral valve indefinitely. I was so relieved. What an amazing surgeon. I had begged him to find another way and he *did*. I started to cry as I thanked him. He went on to explain that my sternum had been opened up twice due to coding and that he literally massaged my heart back to life. He also explained to me that if I chose to litigate, he wouldn't blame me, but he pled his case. I learned that due to the horrendous behavior of the CCU nurses, the entire surgical team would most likely be broken up and possibly even punished for what was done to me, even though they knew nothing about it. So, I thought about it. I couldn't let such a talented group of healers pay a price for something they had nothing to do with. There would be more high-risk patients with families and lives to save. I told the guy who was holding the paperwork to give it to me. I was leafing through it when Bakhos politely asked them to leave. He and I spoke for a few minutes, and then my attorney walked in. I handed him the documents and told him I planned to sign it and to please look it over. He urged me to reconsider; however, I told him no.

"We already have the huge medical malpractice suit going on with Dr. Mengala and the hospital she is with."

I explained to my attorney that my tormenters were never going to care for another patient again, which I thought to be the most important outcome. I told him that I couldn't let the surgical team take that hit. Dr. Bakhos piped in, explaining that there was more information to share. He told me that I would not be charged for the surgery which, even with insurance, would have costed big bucks. He also informed me that any surgical work on my ribs and sternum, which would be needed, would be of no charge. That is when he explained to me how I had multiple broken ribs, some in many places, and that my sternum had splintered. In other words, there would be more shit to deal with. I agreed to the signing of the document to the horror of my attorney, requested to thank the patients who reported it and the nurse who saved me. It was agreed upon, except Dr. Bakhos didn't understand what I meant by "the nurse who saved me." He told me I was found dead on my gurney with my left chest tube rammed into my deflated left lung. I insisted that I was rescued, only to be told that it never happened. So, either I dreamt it all or something very *otherworldly* occurred. After much checking around for a few weeks, I found the answer to be as confusing as the situation. I was adamant to know what happened. I asked my attorney to check it out, and we found that I was correct in my knowledge of being moved to the other CCU. In the report it states that I was found to be "coded" (dead) in the other CCU; however, no one knew how I got there. There was no nurse fitting the description I had given, and it was a mystery to them how I was even moved at all, but I was definitely relocated somehow. The patients who witnessed everything...the ones that reported the abuse, remembered a nurse taking me out of the CCU *before* the code was called. I was quite confused. I say it was an angel...a *real angel*. You guys can come to your own conclusions.

My memory of the time I spent in Loyola healing is random and fractured. The pain from the shattering was so intense that I was under huge doses of Demerol for most of the time. I remember the respiratory therapist coming in and out trying to help me get my left lung back up. I remember a lot of pain and frustration. Finally, when we succeeded, I started walking and doing the stairs until I was able to go home. They took great care of me as I slowly healed, reconstituting my faith in nurses. I was told that I was the *talk* of the hospital. My daily nurses were disgusted by what occurred and were determined to turn it around for me. They were amazing. In no *way* were the two horrific monsters from hell a reflection of the nursing staff at Loyola. I was treated with impeccable care for the remainder of my stay there, and every time since. They were the exceptions to the rule and I…just lucky I guess.

My nurses threw me a little "party" upon my departure; it was sweet of them, and I was SO excited to be going home. Dr. Bakhos tried to explain to me that it will be difficult for me to transition from IV pain meds to pills and that I may go through some withdrawal, but I was far too happy to pay him much mind. Saying he was right and that I should've listened more closely was the understatement of the year.

On our way home, Dan had to pull over several times for me to puke.

I was thrown into drug withdrawal that very day.

For a week I vomited, trembled and dealt with the vicious pain. I twitched and I suffered… all I wanted was to die.

I was left with a healthy respect for *anyone* who endures quitting alcohol and/or drugs without caving. If I had known *anything* about serious street drugs, I probably would have *forced* Dan to go get me some. It was indescribable. I have no words to recount the amount of pain I endured or the power of the cravings for medicine. Again, I just wanted to die.

Our home was a raised ranch. When you enter, there is a foyer and stairs going both up and down. On my first day home, Dan carried me to the stairs and went back to get all the shit in the car. I heard this…river? It was like a sloshing of water onto the walls. It had been raining for days, so I deduced that we had flooded. I figured the sub pump blew and the back-up needed to be plugged in. I figured right. Suddenly, I heard my youngest son Cole holler from downstairs…"I will plug it in, Mom!"

It took a moment to process, but then I screamed, "NO! Cole, NO!"

His answer was, "It's okay! I got it!"

At a loss, I just started swearing. Random cuss words flew out of my mouth like I had Tourette's syndrome. I could hear the sloshing of Coles legs as he made his way to me.

"Mom!" He was confused and a bit frightened.

I held him close and asked, "Honey, were you standing in water when you were going to plug it in?"

His eyes went huge, and he hugged me. I was so grateful. His father walked in, and Cole proudly exclaimed, "Dad! Mom's swearing saved my life!"

Dan looked at us quizzically, and I just shook my head.

"I'll explain it later," I told him.

Cole matter-of-factly added, "Mom, why are you so puffy? Are you going to be fat now?"

Dan and I laughed as he scooped me up and carried me up the stairs. Cole was referring to the bloat throughout my body due to the blood transfusions and plasma products. I was twice my normal size. I looked like Mrs. Stay-puff Marshmallow Woman.

Back in the hospital, when I was just waking, slowly becoming aware of everything after the second heart surgery, I was looking at my arms and my hands. Now, Sissy, my soul sister from Pine Ridge Indian Reservation, had told me that everyone was getting together for a ceremony to make sure my spirit went back into the right body after the surgery. As I looked at the huge swollen arms and fingers, I remember thinking,

AWW SHIT! They messed up the ceremony! I'm in the wrong friggin' body!

The doctors and nurses assured me I was in the correct body and explained that the transfusions caused an immense amount of swelling that would slowly disperse.

SO, back to my first day home...Dan carried me up to the great room, and to my surprise, I saw that the Christmas tree was all set up and decorated. Christmas was only about five days away at this point, and I normally would have panicked immediately had I not come so close to witnessing Cole's demise. Ours was the only house big enough for the whole family to convene in. We hosted *all of the family parties! How* the hell was I going to pull *that* off? Dan explained to me that everyone was coming here to cook, clean, and basically, I would be a guest in my own home. This calmed me down.

The hospital had given us a strange-looking foam thing to put on my bed. It was supposed to help with the pain as the ribs and sternum healed. Neither Dan nor I were sure how it was supposed to be positioned, so I laugh when I think about the many different positions we tried before finally settling on the least painful.

There was no getting comfortable. The pain from my ribs and sternum was intense; my legs ached due to the many blood clots I ended up with from the blood transfusions I required. My head was pounding; I was nauseous and aggravated. Finally, after not being able to get even *close* to comfortable, Dan and I decided to try out the pill medications.

I was amazed at the number of bottles and the size of some of the pills. We dumped the bags of bottles out on the bed and stared at them. Dan diligently looked at my discharge paperwork complete with notes he had taken. I picked up an extremely large bottle containing *ginormous* pills.

"Potassium, hey, check out these bad boys."

He glanced up and widened his eyes. The pills were HUGE.

"Geez," I exclaimed as our eyes met.

I started rummaging through the hoard of plastic containers.

I found one that was labeled "for pain." The bottle read, "Take one pill by mouth every four to six hours as needed for pain."

No, I'm gonna take it by nose,

I thought as I rolled my eyes. I grabbed two of them, because I figured my pain was extra horrible.

"Here's one for muscle cramping," Dan said.

I told him to give me two of those as well. I randomly picked up another bottle.

"Oh! Xanax…I will have two of those, please."

Dan shot me a worried look. I stared back.

"What?!" I challenged him.

"Nothing…" he replied, backing down.

I learned a valuable lesson that evening about the importance of taking my medications responsibly.

After I swallowed all the pills at once, I went back into my room to try to lay down.

I remember this SO clearly, no matter how ridiculous it sounds, it actually happened. Trust me, I was just as freaked out, more so probably…as you will be.

I was laying on my side of the bed and Dan on his. We were watching Dennis Miller on the TV that was mounted up in the corner of the room. Miller cracked a great joke, and I started laughing which was mortifyingly painful. Although the pain was incredible, I couldn't stop laughing… and then coughing. Suddenly I began to feel strange…as if I were floating. I was dizzy…

nauseous, and I closed my eyes. When I opened them next, my back was *stuck* to the ceiling! I know how weird it sounds, but my hand to God, it's the truth. I was *literally* stuck to the ceiling of my bedroom. I could feel my back touching the drywall, and I could see my arms and legs dangling out in front of me; however, I was only able to move my head. I could see Dan laughing at Dennis Miller. I watched myself lying next to him with my eyes closed.

Uh oh…now what's happening?

Whatever was going on, it felt very different from when I was watching my surgery from the corner of the operating room. This time, I intensely wanted to get back into my body; I was actually trying to *push* myself down off the ceiling. A few minutes went by, I saw Dan looking at me on the bed. He first began to shake me gently and then started to panic. I remember trying to answer him, but I couldn't! I was trying to holler out, "I'm on the ceiling! Up here!"

Although the words were coming out of my mouth, it was clear he couldn't hear or see me.

I watched helplessly as he tried to feel for a pulse in my neck. The look on his face was so pathetic and sad that I forged with all my might and somehow made it back into my body. The gasp that came from my mouth sounded as if I had been holding my breath for *way* too long.

"Are you *okay*?" Dan was wide-eyed and horrified.

All I could do was nod my head. He held me and asked, "What happened?!"

I didn't even *try* to explain. I told him he wouldn't believe me if I told him and that I had just better be more careful with those stupid pills. "I was going to say something…" Dan announced.

Later, we checked it out and discovered that I had taken a fatal dose of oxycontin unintentionally. I wanted the pain to go away or at least get *a lot* better, so I doubled my dose and added a couple of muscle relaxers and a Xanax or two. To this day I am sure I was on my "way out"…. through the ceiling.

I cried throughout most of the first few days, taking breaks when the boys and/or friends and relatives were there. When people finally quit "stopping by," I hit the bed and balled my eyes out like a baby. I was certifiable. I was telling Dan to hold me, and the next minute I was cussing and pushing him away. I couldn't move my arms properly, and it was pissing me off incredibly. I was wearing what the osteopaths refer to as "the cage" around my shattered ribs and sternum which was wired together and not yet fused. I still had that intense pain coming from inside my body that I *thought* was from the kidney infarct.

The healing process from all of this was grueling. I had to choose between enduring incredible pain or feeling like I was down the rabbit hole with Alice. I was going back and forth to the different doctors dealing with my post-surgical non-union and the ribs that didn't want to heal. The infection along with the scraping had done a real number on my body, causing random sharp organ pains and leaving me weak and nauseous. These were the most miserable days so far and I remember thinking,

Well, it can't get any worse…

Boy, was I wrong. Yes, the dominos *were* falling, but they were far from finished. They were just getting started.

OH, ooooooooooh, dominoooooooo

Time *dragged* on as I dealt with each internal issue at a time. Nephrologists, otolaryngologists, osteopaths, cardiologists, hematologists, infectious disease, osteopaths, monthly labs, and more. I remember being irrationally afraid that the infection would come back. I still felt so weak and helpless. Every movement was a struggle. I constantly wanted to sleep; however, the nightmares of the "evil nurses" were always waiting for me.

It was a "no brainer" that I needed a new ob-gyn doctor, and after much research, I began to see Dr. Melvin Gerbie at Northwestern. I had heard of him multiple times from others when telling my story. I was impressed and decided to choose him for my pelvic care physician. Despite my burgeoning fear of doctors, I went for a consult and immediately adored him. He had such an amazing personality and seemed genuinely horrified to hear about what I had gone through so far. Doctor Gerbie was amazed about the entire situation and had a theory about the pelvic pain I was still suffering. It may have taken a while, but he finally convinced me into an exploratory surgery to validate his theory. He cut me from the belly button to the pelvic mound and inspected the area. After viewing the damage done by the first "doctor," fixing what he could, he performed a biopsy of an "unidentifiable mass" on my bladder. This, I believe saved my life once again, because he found that the biopsy revealed this mass to be my fallopian tube! Had that gone unnoticed and untreated, the infection would have most definitely returned and killed me. The doctors at

Northwestern were amazed that it *hadn't* already returned. I remember being told that it was a miracle they cured the infection with that condition actively working against it. The rogue tube was serving as a conduit for bacteria that eventually would have killed me. This was a particularly difficult piece of knowledge to wrap my head around. What was Dr. Mengala *thinking?* All I can come up with is that she was hoping I would just die and that no one would ever find out about the tube she dropped. At any time, she could have told someone (anyone) about the situation and helped to resolve it. She did nothing. I lingered cluelessly in constant pain while *she* silently knew that my right tube was lost *somewhere* in my body. I think back on *that* and wonder why I didn't have her arrested for attempted murder!

Dr. Gerbie explained the results of the biopsy to me. He told me that the stabbing abdominal pain was due to my fallopian tube having been *plunged* into my bladder, the other end jutting out vaginally. He performed *another* hysterectomy and removed the mangled tube, part of my bladder, and part of my vagina.

Gee, thanks Dr. Mengala. You shit-stain.

I was beyond angry when Dr. Gerbie told me how my organs were all "scraped up" and traumatized. He discerned that Mengala must have dropped the tube and searched everywhere for it, causing an amazing amount of scar tissue. I was so full of hate and dismay that I felt as though the steam could be *seen* coming out of my ears. I was an emotional train wreck at this point.

The lawsuit kicked into high gear upon the revelation of the fallopian tube's presence. Dr. Gerbie shot up as our *key* witness for the trial. He immediately agreed to testify fully, as he was horrified that it had occurred in the first place. Dr. Melvin Gerbie is another "healer/doctor" like Dr. Baggs. A true hero, in it for the right reasons.

Although we were all horrified, my attorney told me that now we can actually *prove* that the infection was due to negligence and an abandonment of the proper standards of medical care. If I was supposed to be happy about it, I failed miserably. I was lost and confused. I couldn't stop wondering *why* she didn't just TELL me. My head felt so messed up from this alone that it was difficult for me to get past it. I was still having nightmares about the sadist nurses from hell, genuinely horrified that drug abuse victims were being treated that way by them. I worried about people I didn't even *know*, wondering how many "nurses" like that were actually out there. It frightened me that one doctor could be so wonderful, and another, so cruel. Same with the nurses. I found it mind blowing; the dichotomy of the kindness and the evil that was out there when one was most vulnerable. Never before was I treated even *closely* to what I went through with those horrible women. To the contrary, actually. Being in the hospital so often, nurses were a constant in my life, and I loved every one of the rest of them. I became close with several who are still my friends to this day.

Despite the impeccable care I received from then on, I was always scared to death while under the care of *anyone*. I trusted *no one*. Once bitten and all.

I must say though that in general, my nurses were like angels to me throughout the rest of my maladies. I never would have made it through it if it weren't for their nurturing kindness and impeccable care. I believe nurses are angels in disguise, and rarely but once in a million times…*demons*.

As the lawsuit forged on, my attorney was waiting impatiently for the pathology results from the first hysterectomy. It was requested quite early on but was still not a part of the file. The pathology results from the *second* hysterectomy were in before the first which was a year and a half earlier. One day, though, he called to let me know it had finally arrived. He asked me if I was sitting down.

Oh great, here we go again. Now what?

He proceeded to explain to me that the results from pathology showed a perfectly *normal* uterus. There was no infection, no signs of endometriosis or any other kind of uterine disease. She took out a perfectly good uterus that may have given me a daughter one day. I was so disgusted that I literally put the phone down to go vomit. He also explained that there was no right fallopian tube included in the pathology samples.

To this very *day* I cannot comprehend why this "doctor" did what she did. She convinced me that my normal uterus was in need of being removed or I may die and preceded to botch the surgery up, deciding not to tell anyone what had occurred in the operating room. Trial depositions and testimonies from the nurses would reveal that they were sworn to secrecy and even threatened with their jobs. The whole thing blew my mind. Here I was, physically *shaking* with the desire to beat the hell out of Dr. Mengala and I couldn't even tie my own shoes.

Looking back, I can see how the anger limited me from progressing medically. I was so full of hate and ridiculously tensed up all the time that I was unable to even contemplate my options and/or issues. The knowledge that there were people out there who actually behaved the way Mengala and her minions did simply *amaze* me. I wanted to go on a personal quest to search them all out and make things right. I was far too busy *surviving*, though to do more than just think about it. It was beyond frustrating.

Prior to the trial, there were *many large* settlement offers. I have to admit that the money was tempting; however, I wanted her license to *operate*. *That* they kept taking off the table. I decided to go to trial. I figured I am up to my neck in it so far…may as well dunk my head in.

My attorney had worked his ass off and was now ready. He patiently explained to me each portion of the trial. To say I was "interested" just doesn't cover it…I was fascinated by the whole thing. From the pre-trial process of "motions Illimani" and the "voir dire" of the jury to the complicated medical testimonies, I acquired quite the legal/medical education.

The trial was in its infancy the day I realized I was being followed. At first, I thought I was just paranoid, but slowly, it became obvious. Everywhere I went, there was the same unfamiliar car, with the same man in it, taking pictures of me. I wasn't doing much driving, but when I *could*, I would see him following me around. He was about as inconspicuous as a bleeding sow in the snow. One time, just to mess with him, I ditched him, went around the back and pulled up behind, scaring the *hell* out of him. That was a good day. But most days were not good days. Most days I felt miserable from the pain, anxious to the point of extreme paranoia and worried that I wouldn't get a fair trial. I had turned down a few very high offers, and I kept thinking,

What if I end up with nothing?

The trial was scheduled to go down in the *big* courtroom at DuPage County courthouse in Wheaton, Illinois. The first time I saw it all set up was frightening. There were many observers which I found strange. Later, I would learn that the majority of the onlookers were students and a few lawyers. The man representing Mengala's insurance company was there, and I could *feel* his eyes all over me constantly. Foolishly, I thought that my family and friends would be in the audience; however, most were set to testify and prohibited from sitting in on the proceedings prior to their testimony. They were allowed to attend trial *after* they testified but were not allowed in until then.

I felt very vulnerable and alone. I always tried not to look at the jury, but that's a difficult thing to accomplish. It constantly seemed as if at least *one* of the twelve were looking at me, and I couldn't help looking back. It was an uncontrollable impulse.

The trial took a smidge over two weeks. My testimony alone took almost a week; the attorneys on the other side trying desperately to discredit me. I remember one morning I walked into the nearly empty courtroom early to find a projector displaying a *huge* image of me protesting at an Indian rights rally. I had my friend Carla's baby in my arms as I marched with my fist up and a ridiculous grimace on my face. The image was larger than life, and I gawked at it absurdly. When Gary, my attorney, walked in, he shook his head and told me not to worry about it. He said they are just trying to get the jury to dislike you. In the picture you could see that I was wearing a "camp justice" T-shirt toting Casper, my friend's bi-racial baby boy. Oh yes, DuPage County was extremely conservative and judgmental…they used this to their advantage as they paraded pictures of my protesting. They were trying to portray me as a troublemaker, a *radical*, and it was working. As the trial went on, fewer and fewer jurors looked at me nicely, if at all. I could tell that they hated me. I could *feel* it. Our judge could feel it as well.

The last day of closing arguments before the jury was to convene, my judge called a meeting in her chambers.

She met with me alone at first, later bringing in the rest of the key players. I remember her calming smile as she explained to me that she felt "uncomfortable" to let those twelve people decide the outcome due to the fact that this case was extremely complicated. She thought it best for all of us to come to some kind of compromise. Right then and there, before I left empty-handed. I asked her *why* she felt that way and cried as she explained that she could just *tell* that they weren't going to give me much, if *anything*, and that there was no WAY I was going to get her license to operate which was my biggest goal. I didn't want her doing this to anybody else…or anyone else's wife, daughter, mother, etc.

Needless to say, I was crushed. I kept asking her "WHY?!"

She tried to explain, but honestly, to this day, I still do not fully understand.

Tort reform was in the news daily, speaking to how frivolous lawsuits were chasing away all of the good doctors in Illinois. The county was split but much heavier on the conservative side. My lawyer did a great job proving that Mengala and her boyfriend were menaces to patients; however, according to my judge, I wasn't injured badly enough. I remember thinking…

Are they serious?

The problem seemed to stem from the fact that I was still walking and talking. I wasn't disfigured (yet); I wasn't in a wheelchair; I didn't walk with a cane…the jury thought we were exaggerating. This blew my mind. I had fabulous expert witnesses along with cold hard facts to back up everything I endured and how it actually…*literally* killed me several times. However, I *wasn't* dead now. Wrongful death suits brought more money than medical malpractice ones. I was disgusted.

We stayed late into the night bickering back and forth about money, consequences, and non-disclosure riders… I refused to *budge* when it came to her license to operate. After intense negotiations, we finally settled. I took a lot less money than I should have, but I got her license. After all was said and done, I ended up with a little under a million dollars and her license. She could still deliver babies, but she could no longer perform hysterectomies. Also, her malpractice insurance would be astronomical from then on. I really liked that part. I was satisfied that she couldn't do this to anybody else. Her lawyers diligently strived to get me to sign a non-disclosure agreement, a document that said I wasn't allowed to speak of the situation or write about it. I knew I was going to tell the world somehow, so I refused to sign it. More money was taken from the offer.

While I was still suffering post open-heart, way prior to the trial, I received a phone call from Oprah Winfrey's producer. They were doing a show on medical mishaps and wanted me to be on it. I really wanted to do it; however, my attorney wouldn't even consider it.

"No way," he told me. "It will compromise the case."

The opposing council must have heard about that because they really wanted that non-disclosure agreement signed. I refused and never signed it, even as they kept whittling money off the offer. How could I? I felt that I had a responsibility to tell people what was going on out there. A *duty* to warn you guys!

After the trial, I tried my best to get back to normal. I began playing softball again, riding horses, working and volunteering as I had done before; however, I was in constant pain. I had to *teach* myself how to move differently… *properly* without causing pain. Some things that are usually so mundane…like sneezing, were torturous. I couldn't sleep without Xanax, and I couldn't get out of bed without heavy duty pain meds. I walked around doing my routine like a malfunctioning "Stepford" wife. Each day, all day, was a reminder of everything that had happened. When I *could* sleep, I would have night terrors.

In these nightmares, the setting was a medieval dungeon, and I was bound with chains to a hospital gurney as the evil nurses tortured me. Most nights I would wake up spittin' mad and sweating heavily; some nights, the angel who saved me would *again*…save me. Some nights not. Either way, I would wake up traumatized and in crises. I suffered many panic attacks, and I developed an abhorrence of hospitals, doctors, surgeries, and even lab tests. I was laden with anxiety on the days I had anything medically related to attend to, which was almost every day. I spoke very little about the entire situation to others, and I slept as much as possible.

I went through pleurisy, pneumonia twice and walked around with ribs that were technically still broken and a hole in my sternum. I went for unusually painful shots to the sternum to promote healing. The needle looked like a *joke* it was so big! Like a prop from a cartoon!

There were days I *couldn't* get out of bed, days I simply didn't *want to*, and days where I would venture out to the local grocery store or take a short walk. Any of the above referenced activities caused great pain and exhausted me to the point of literally passing out several times. Once, right in the store.

I was adamant to get my life back to normal yet freakishly afraid someone would hug me too hard or that I may trip and fall. Riding horses was so painful that I rarely did it anymore. It was crazy. I forged on, though, figuring things would get better as time went on. Yeah, right.

Dan and I basically put four walls around the money we received by purchasing a warehouse fit for a proper pool company. Foolishly, we underestimated the freakishly high Cook County taxes and failed to factor in the market crash. The excess overhead we incurred was far higher than we figured it to be. I also bought a horse, because I was so stubborn to return to normal. We gave each family member five thousand dollars as a token of our love and appreciation, paid what medical bills we could, which basically used up all of the money we had received

I diligently went to and from doctor appointments and physical therapy. I thought I was on my way to getting my life back. Except for the pain, everything seemed to be falling into place like finally finishing a large and difficult puzzle. I thought I was putting the last piece in place when suddenly I received a disturbing phone call.

I will never forget *that phone call*. I have nightmares about it, just like the nurse tormentors, and they don't feel like nightmares at all. I actually don't think that they *are* nightmares. I believe they are memories that refuse to go away, hijacking you when you're sleeping.

I was alone in the house, preparing for a softball game and changing out of my work clothes, when the phone rang. I almost didn't answer it, because I didn't recognize the number. I distinctly remember that I was looking for my other softball spike (shoe). The woman on the other end asked to speak to me to which I replied she already was. She didn't ask me if I was sitting down or if I was alone in the house…she simply and quite mundanely told me that I had breast cancer and I needed to call the surgeon and the oncology department for appointments immediately. I was on the stairs when she told me; I remember my legs going weak and almost falling down. Thankfully, my son Jesse came walking in the door and immediately rushed to my side and wanted to know what was going on.

I had a couple of lumpectomies done over the years, all showing pre-cancer, but I was firmly against a mastectomy. I tried in vain to "save the girls." I was forced to get mammograms done every three months. I never even entertained the idea that I would actually *get* breast cancer as I figured I had gone through enough and that would just be…I don't know, *unfair?* Well, so much for positive thinking.

Jesse held me steady as he walked me up the stairs to the couch. He phoned his father, and I sat there in shock for a while thinking,

No…this has GOT to be a mistake.

At my oncology appointment with the surgeon, I was told that I had stage 3 IDC on the right side and thirteen pre-cancerous calcifications on the left. He advised a bi-lateral radical mastectomy as the calcifications would most likely become cancerous over time. We discussed the surgery and reconstruction process, and I remember imagining it all and thinking,

But my chest hurts constantly!

I couldn't even *fathom* how I was going to get through this one.

If someone even ventured too closely to my ribs or sternum, I would back away protectively…and they're planning to do *what?*

Aww, man, no way.

I underwent the mastectomy and reconstruction, while suffering from incredible chest pain. I felt as if I were in a dream for most of the breast cancer treatment, going to and from Northwestern in and out of treatment.

Although I felt horrible all of the time, I was attempting, yet again, to get back into my life when I passed out and was rushed to Northwestern emergency room. I woke up to what at first I thought to be a nightmare…nurses, doctors, tubes, and beeping.

OH NO. Not again…

At the start of this *new* affliction, I was too busy vomiting and passing out to know what was happening. I felt like I was dying again. As the doctors strived to get the steroids balanced properly, I was told that I have advanced Addison's disease complicated by a hyper thyroid. The general consensus was that the treatment for the cancer had killed my adrenal glands. Because a *total* loss of adrenal function is very rare; a woman came all the way from the Mayo clinic to speak to me about it… She represented an Addison's awareness group. She tried to prepare me for what I was going to endure.

Basically, she explained that I would *always* feel like I had the flu.

Just Lovely.

We discussed the importance of keeping the steroids balanced properly and what to expect if they were *not.* She was adamant that I carry an EPI pen.

Dutifully, and feeling very much like a monkey in a lab, I listened to her whole "spiel" and said very little. I thought,

I'm done fighting. I got nothing left.

Conquered. I had no more energy to even *try* to fight. When the woman left my room, I couldn't even cry. I was so pissed off. There were too many dominos falling, and I just couldn't keep up with them. I kept hearing that song in my head…

Oh, Oh, Domino…Roll me over; Romeo; there you go.

I now think back to that time, and I just shake my head. Each time I was certain that it couldn't *possibly* get any worse, I was wrong.

Although I fiercely fought through my maladies with my head down pushing through the bullshit, I eventually ended up with several more "conditions," one leaving me horribly disfigured. It felt as though I was being *punished* for something. It was as if I was "doing time" for a crime I didn't commit.

Each day was a study in endurance. I forced myself to get through it, sometimes literally fainting from exhaustion. I wanted SO badly to be "normal" again. My life was filled with appointments, tests, procedures, and surgeries. The medication the doctors had me on for the pain and anxiety made it difficult to think, and I grudgingly left the important business decisions to Dan. I no longer trusted my own thought process. Clearing doorways was about the best I could do. I didn't even feel "human" anymore.

My immune system was so depleted that I was forever sick...like the snotty kid in class. I kept trying to lower my medication due to the fact that I was a literal zombie at times; however, *that* would cause even *more* issues. I thought I would never get used to life this way and just wanted to move on. I was paranoid of everything...nothing *felt* normal, and I grew increasingly more sick and tired of life. My friends, thinking I was merely "depressed," attempted to get me out of the house, but I could only last a couple of hours before I insisted upon going home. Each day I looked forward to the end of it, a day was just something to get through...sleep was my only relief. Sweet, wonderful, painless sleep. I spent more days *in* bed than *out* of bed, and I felt as though I was decomposing while still alive.

It was the flesh-eating viral infection on my *face* that was the straw that broke the camel's back.

One day, seemingly out of nowhere, my face was covered in deep, ulcerative, painful wounds that felt like burns and refused to heal. It looked like leprosy to me. The feeling was similar to a *biting* or stinging of some type. My face was cracking and bleeding spontaneously, and I was unable to face the world. I was certain that I was losing my mind. The dermatologists I saw constantly wanted to biopsy every wound from this mystery skin disease. They found malignant melanoma on my face in *one* biopsy, thus encouraging them to biopsy every wound that came up. By the time dermatology was through with me, I looked like a road map of facial scars. I was able to hide all of my other scars beneath my clothes, but now what?

A paper bag over my head?

I had enough. No more biopsies, no more surgeries; I was suffering from medical post-traumatic stress syndrome and had picked up an irrational fear of doctors and hospitals. I couldn't even visit loved ones if they were in a hospital. I would suffer a panic attack every time I tried. My doctors didn't really want me in a hospital anyways, being that I caught *everyone's everything*. Throughout the entire ordeal, there were years that I spent more time *in* the hospital than *out*.

Life was kicking my ass. Every time I got *up*, it smacked me around some more and threw me back to the ground.

I worked hard on "carrying on" while being in never-ending pain *and* feeling as if I had the flu every day; I was doing well if you didn't count crying myself to sleep almost every night.

When the Addison's disease was at its worst, before the steroids were balanced properly, I would randomly awaken to find myself in the hospital after suffering what they call an "Addisonian crises." Once I was sure I wasn't having a nightmare, I would get angry. I just couldn't figure out what to do to become "normal" again. My doctors were very proud of me…some giving me names like Humpty Dumpty and others calling me a miracle. Funny, I didn't *feel* like a miracle. I felt like a southbound runaway train wreck. Humpty Dumpty was far more fitting.

One day, confined to my hospital bed, my mind wandered. Many thoughts skimmed the edge of my consciousness; however, there was one that persisted. How could SO much have happened to one person, and WHY was that person me? Was I *Hitler* in a past life? Even more annoying was why, after thirty-five years of metamorphosis … transforming nearly EVERYTHING about myself that I hated, do I still not *like* myself enough to get past the scars and physical deformities I have been left with? When I look into a mirror, why am I so perplexed? I think, who *is* this person? Instead of celebrating my victorious battles, I felt beaten down. I had lost my will to fight like an exhausted boxer taking the knockout punch deliberately. At the mirror I would think, who *is* this person?

I *feel* like the same person on the inside…but looking back at myself from the glass stands a complete stranger. It makes me wonder if I had ever even been *acquainted* with who I truly am inside! Prior to my medical mayhem, had the person I thought I knew to be me been told that one day I would fight an epic battle…many in fact, that I would emerge victorious; however, I would be physically transformed into a hideous looking monster, and there won't be a damn thing I can do about it… I would have NEVER even considered the possibility that I would shrink and cave. *That* person…the one I *thought* to be me would have said something to the effect of

Well, at least I survived it!

Who cares what I look like?

If people stared at me or said cruel things, "*SHE*" would word whip their asses to show them how their superficiality is more a negative reflection on THEMSELVES than her. I was convinced that it wouldn't bother me at all. That's what I did when *strangers* were being cruelly stared at in my presence. It was one of the only things I did *well*…word whipping the rude… How frightening it is to realize that my "bravado" was just bullshit hiding behind the protection of a normal, not-too-ugly face. Wow. I was ashamed and disappointed in myself. Was I a snowflake? Did they kill the old me? Either that or I must not have even *known* myself at all. When I was still healthy, had someone asked me how I would handle this very situation…I would confidently expect the polar opposite of how I actually *am* handling it.

So, what does *that* mean? Did I overestimate my spiritual strength *then*, or have I transformed into the superficial coward I am today, and if so, why? Why, when young and not so ugly, did I insist that I felt uncomfortable being stared at by strangers only to now turn into a *mess* when stared at because I am facially disfigured? I think I actually remember saying something to the equivalent of "I hate the staring! I am sure they wouldn't be ogling me like this if I were ugly or *deformed* in some way!"

Oh, yes, I was sure that I would LOVE to be in the position to tell these people off. I believe I even went so far as to say, "I wish I *was* maimed, and that they were staring at THAT! It would be better than this, and I would REALLY tell these people OFF!"

Yeah, right…here I am, IN the situation I basically ASKED for, and I panic when stared at. I hide in my house for the most part, but if I DO get ambitious enough to leave, I am a social train wreck. Had I *truly* been the pillar of inspiration thought to be by those closest to me and those who sought my council…I would hold my head up and *educate* the ignorant. I used to believe, that because I bravely jumped in to protect those who were being bullied and rudely questioned *or* even *stared at* about their differences, that if I were to be disfigured in some way I would surely emerge proud and strong against the same. I do not know if I am just crushingly disappointed at my inner-self or if I had been this vain, this super-fucking-ficial all along. What happened to that twenty-something-year-old spitfire who would pounce on the first asshole to ridicule *anyone*, let alone someone suffering from a medical issue? Did life turn me into a spineless coward *as well* as a hideous beast? I just don't get it. Rationally…intellectually, I *KNOW*… am aware of the fact, that I must rise above the judgement…face the invasive ignorance, yet I cannot. So, what is it then? Did my enormous ego create a fictitious "me" in order to *like* myself? Well, if that was the plan, I couldn't have failed more miserably…when I first became ill, I could not *STAND* myself. I knew that if I were to stay sane throughout my reclusive and lonely diseases, I would not only need to get a few things straight with myself…I would need to *change* completely! Oh, man, it was like being assigned the roommate from *HELL* in prison…like being put at the foot of Mt. Everest barefooted in a storm and forced to summit! Surely, I could NOT do this, I thought. I was SO disappointed in myself for turning out to be a vain, superficial hypocrite. I struggled intensely with just how the hell was I going to turn this around.

The journey began with one step, as most journeys do. It is the digging in and acquiring purchase that truly inspired me to climb on. There were avalanches to get through and crevasses to carefully navigate over, but each small accomplishment…each bit of traction, served as an incentive to continue. I did not summit the mountain on my first attempt…nor my second. I can't even *count* the number of tries it took to even *see* its majestic peak let alone to *conquer* it. Eventually, though, I *did* summit. I had a lot of help…so much so that I actually deserve the *least* amount of credit out of everyone. They ought to give out awards to the family members who become caregivers. These thankless heroes are lost in the whole "who's the victim" bullshit when someone becomes permanently ill or disabled.

In my opinion, right out of the gate I say *they* are more selfless by the mere fact that they have a CHOICE in the matter! When life messes you up, you no longer have the *luxury* once afforded. Those who take on the responsibility of becoming caregivers, and even more so, those who stick around when the going not only gets tough, it gets *im-fucking-POSSIBLE*...they are the heroes. I have heard many stories of marriages either *ending* or drastically deteriorating once an illness has joined the relationship. I guess I got lucky. Each time I was going down, my husband Dan caught me just before I face-planted. He held me up, and we kind of merged into one. Dan did a *lot* of carrying me. We were fortunate that I was small and he, strong.

♫ *Oh, oh, domino...Roll me over, Romeo...*
There you go...dig it! I said Ohh ohhhh Domino...

When I finally got over the disfigurement, life really got difficult. I had no idea, as I was pre-occupied with survival and a hideous face, that my oldest son, Jesse was on a fast joyride headed straight for a cliff.

Dan had done his best with everything on his overfilled plate; however, Jesse snuck under the radar and was getting involved with all the wrong people and situations.

I remember way back to when I was released from the hospital after the heart surgeries. I was trying to get comfortable in my bed when Jesse came into my room, kissed me, and said, "Bye, Mama, see ya later."

Now, this was at 9:00 P.M. on a school night, and my son was twelve years old. I told him he was going *nowhere* except bed and he protested, arguing, "Dad lets me! This is how we do things now!"

I told him to get his ass in his room and get ready for bed. I had no idea of the epic battle that was brewing. I explained to him that I was back and that the party was over. Ah, that it were that easy! After everything I thought was so horrible that had happened, I learned that all of that was *nothing* compared to the helplessness of watching your first-born son ruin his life.

As if skyscrapers in an earthquake, the dominos were still falling...

They were actually picking up speed instead of coming to a stop. It is mind-blowing how one evil decision made on the part of an unethical doctor could cause such devastating repercussions. It was one thing to mess *me* up… but now it was affecting my family. Dan had done a magnificent job caring for *everything* throughout our nightmare; however, Jesse creatively cruised under his radar. He is a very crafty boy.

When I became ill, my boys, for the first time, tasted sweet freedom from authority. Cole would sneak disgusting video games at home, and Jesse began hanging around some seriously scary people. By the time Dan and I figured it all out, Jesse had become a full-fledged menace to society…a *gang member*. Following in the footsteps of one of his newfound friends. This was no joke as we lived in Chicago and kids died on the streets here every day. We lived in a pretty sub-division near O'Hare airport; however, we were mere minutes away from the frightening west side of Chicago. Most people think that the "south side" of Chicago is the worst, but it's not…the west side is far more dangerous. The gangs were fighting over drug sale territories and moving into the near western suburbs, using recruits, young and innocent boys, to do their dirty work. Most often they would get the kids hooked on drugs, but I was lucky Jesse never really got "into" doing them. He was, however, pulled in by the comradery and danger. Jesse had always been a risk taker…an adrenaline lover. I hate to admit it, but he gets that from me. Prior to settling down, I lived my life as though I was invincible. I jumped out of a perfectly good airplane multiple times and loved it! I went on one-hundred-mile, week long, endurance horse rides on the reservation every year, The Crazy Horse Ride. Even after my multiple medical issues, I pushed myself to complete the ride each year. Some years I was successful, others I was not. Either way, I was always pushing myself. However, in my youth, I was always trying new and exciting things.

Not far from the ranch that I would ride at was a big cat sanctuary, The Valley of The Kings. I would volunteer there as often as I could. I loved getting up close and personal with the animals. There weren't just large wild cats; they also had a grizzly bear named Archie who we fed peanut butter and jelly sandwiches to and a beautiful pack of wolves that had an amazing amount of room to roam, all fenced in and served as a perimeter around the property. Occasionally the alarm would go off if an animal got out; however, the knowledgeable staff would handle it. Those few residents nearby knew about the alarm and cooperated well. I loved it there. I loved everything about it except the smell. It wasn't open to the public; however, if you gave a substantial donation, you could get a tour of the facility. I was a volunteer and would help with feeding; the sanctuary went through an amazing amount of food! The local authorities would drop off roadkill at the gate, and we would drag it back for the lions and tigers. Feeding time was a trip though! We would coerce the large cats into a separate area of the enclosure, put the meat into the main area, get out and let them back in. An interesting side-note: Unable to use food to coerce them into a holding area without creating fights, the handlers used carpet fresh powder! I shit you not! For some reason they were highly attracted to it and would roll around and play in it as we pulled the meat into the main area. Because all the large males were kept in the same huge enclosure, to be stuck in there at feeding time would mean certain death. I loved it and went as often as I could, even between medical maladies.

One day, after I had finally started to feel well enough to run around on my own, I received a text from a fellow volunteer.

"We need to put Kokie Joe down for dental work today; if you want to pet him or anything, get your ass over here."

Needless to say, I jumped at the chance and drove out there. When I arrived, my friend Kierra grabbed me and hurried me into the infirmary. There was Joe…one of the largest tigers in the sanctuary. He was relatively new from Bengal, India and devastatingly beautiful. After being assured by the vet that he was "totally out," Kierra and I petted him, checked out his huge paws, and just before leaving, we snuggled our faces into his soft neck fur. It was an amazing experience, and I will never forget it. How *could* I? The consequences are all over my *face!*

It wasn't long before I was again too sick to work at the ranch, ride horses, and volunteer at the sanctuary. This is how I believe I acquired the skin disease.

A few weeks later, Kierra rode my horse in a barrel competition and did really well. She called to thank me, and we started chatting. She told me about this strange skin problem she was having. I felt so bad for my beautiful young friend. It was only about a week after the call that I began to have the exact same skin symptoms as she.

My face began to tingle and itch. It felt as though I had bugs crawling under my skin. These were the same issues my friend had described to me. One morning, I awoke to blood on my pillow. Going to mirror, I saw what looked to be a small, bleeding, for lack of a better word… *lightning bolt* on my face. The wound was linear, like a small Z. It was as if my face was having an earthquake…*skinquake?* The crazy part was how *painful* it was. It felt more like a burn than a cut. There were pieces of what at first I thought to be glass, coming out of the wound. These were tiny, fiber-like strings of different colors that were stiff and sharp like glass. I immediately sought out a dermatologist. More accurately, I sought out *scads* of dermatologists. I saw nine different ones resulting in no relief. My condition just continued to get worse. Having been quite active, I had suffered *many* cuts before; however, these lesions were different. They would sting like burns and relentlessly throb from pain. They never quite healed, they would merely get better and worse. I was crazy from the dynamic pain and could only deal with them if they were covered with a local pain-relieving ointment. I ran around with Band-Aids on my face everywhere. I wanted to leave the wounds open to dry and heal, but I could not handle the pain. They would spontaneously bleed, often causing my day to be spent tending to them. I would have a blood-soaked rag to my face, constantly applying pressure to stop the bleeding. Each day I was more horrified than the last as I watched my once normal skin splitting apart before my very eyes.

The dermatologists would give different diagnoses. The only thing they seemed to agree upon was that it was referred to as "Morgellon's disease." Now there were two schools of thought on this "Morgellon's disease"… one was that it was all psychological and should be treated as delirious dermatitis, and the other, that it was an unknown parasitic disease. Whatever it is; I am not alone in my suffering. Upon delving into the world wide web, I learned that thousands of people, mostly middle-aged women, were also dealing with this relentless affliction. Try as I might, I could not find a common denominator amongst the suffering except that we were all experiencing the same symptoms, most were women, and that they all had another underlying medical issue. After years of research, my opinion is that it is a microscopic parasite that afflicts women with suppressed or compromised immune systems and at rare times, men.. The Addison's disease I acquired is an autoimmune affliction and I constantly tested borderline for lupus, convincing my doctors that I probably *did* have that as well. They prescribed me more steroids.

Hurray.

It is difficult to adequately describe the horror my life had turned into. Not only was I caught up in a tsunami of doctors, treatments, and misery. I was now watching my eldest son Jesse ruin his life. I cried myself to sleep most nights; my salty tears of self-pity causing even more pain as they stung the wounds on my swollen face. I couldn't win for losing, and I began to give up right about then. I felt as though I had nothing left. I had existed for my boys. Fighting for my life was all about watching them grow up and thrive. At this point, however, all I was watching was the morning news to make sure Jesse didn't get *shot* the night before. He had turned into a rough and tumble thug right before my eyes. There were nights he came home bleeding…beaten. He would never allow me to help him with his wounds, thus I never really knew what they were. My sweet baby boy had become a total stranger to me, seemingly overnight. Dan and I tried *everything* to change his behavior: pulled him out of the public school and scraped to send him to a private high school, there were councilors, interventions, boundaries, and consequences for violating them. We were constantly on him about curfew, if he even came home at all. I prayed every night that he would abandon his newfound lifestyle and clean up his act. Thankfully, he did. We never gave up on him as he turned his life around. It was another epic battle, this time I was fighting for the life of my son, though…his future. His father and I helped him get through jail stays and his legal troubles, but that is another book entirely. We suffered financially due to attorney bills and also emotionally as the gang activity ramped up. They buffeted my home with bullets and once actually gained entry, shooting and killing my beloved dog. I have no words for the grief I experienced from that.

I am proud to say that my Jesse is now a law-abiding, hard-working family man who stays far from trouble. He found love, our Amanda, and has been transformed. His days are consumed with work and his evenings are for his children, my beautiful and amazing grandchildren. All evidence that love works. Pure, unconditional love can conquer anything.

Some nights, I dream of running across the ocean shore on horseback, playing softball and/or skiing. I wake with such joy, only to be reminded that it was just a dream. That is like staring down a long, dark train tunnel and seeing a light at the end of it. The happiness would drain from my body as soon as I realized that the light I could see at the end…was from another train heading straight for me!

With a long list of disabilities piling up, each new revolting development would come complete with a new doctor, a new treatment, pill, surgery, or lifestyle change. I must admit I pretty much held it together until the dermatology department insisted that I was cutting my face with a razor. That threw me into an intense rant which caused me to be prohibited from that floor of the professional building. I still say it was uncalled for on their part. It is an amusing letter to read, but definitely…uncool.

After nine dermatologists, I decided to learn to care for my skin condition on my own. I knew I wasn't causing these wounds and I wanted them to be gone. I researched how to rid one's self of a parasite and religiously followed the routine. Finally, after years of constant trial and error, I began to see some progress…some of the wounds were healing! I doubled my daily doses of vitamins, pumpkin seeds, and frozen lemon peel and found that, slowly, I was finally winning. There were scars where the wounds had erupted; however, there seemed to be less and less new wounds as time went on. I took dozens of vitamins and supplements, each having its own way of helping to achieve the common goal…getting rid of the parasites. I was overjoyed to see that all of this was actually working. Each day my skin seemed to get a little better. I eyed the "light at the end of the tunnel" suspiciously but continued fighting, bracing myself for another catastrophe the whole time.

Most of the money we received from the lawsuit went to purchasing a huge warehouse for our pool company. This would allow us to purchase material at a much better price in bulk and to have plenty of room to stock up on parts. The front of the warehouse was a small office equipped with three work areas and a small sitting area for perspective customers. Not realizing the amount of overhead and taxes we were incurring, we operated through lines of credit. We kept our credit perfect in order to protect these essential lifelines. Then, in 2008 the stock market tanked, and the banks started pulling our lines of credit one by one. Our perfect score meant nothing…the banks were tumbling and snatching back the credit they once threw at us. We were forced to operate using our own capital, and we began to struggle. The pool business generates a lot of money; however, it also sucks that money up incredibly fast. Each week was (and is) a struggle to make bank for payroll. Our customers were hit hard by the recession as well, and it suddenly became far more difficult to collect money. Suppliers were going out of business, and there was a lull in the new builds. It was a frightening time for us. We braced ourselves, thinking we would have to close our doors. We made it through that horrible time; I don't know *how*, but we did. It took blood, sweat, tears, and every cent we had left, but it was worth it.

As I sit here now, February 2020, I think back to the storms we endured… the hell we went through as a family, and I am thankful for every moment of it. Were it not to have been, I would not be the person I am today. Yes, we fight for our victories and mourn our losses, yet all of these experiences create the people we become. The pain makes our bodies stronger. The misery grants us compassion and empathy towards others, and the heartaches encourage us to fight harder for what we love. I now feel more like our Country did post 911. Tragic, yes, but proud of the way we rallied together as a people.

I used to think about what my life would be like if none of this had occurred. Now, I try not to look back…that's not the way I am headed…I am going forward into a new phase of my life. Writing this book was extremely cathartic for me. With every key stroke I made peace with the past and am now forging into the future. Thank you for reading; I hope you all have seen my mistakes and learn from them. Had I pursued a second opinion on the hysterectomy, none of this would have ever happened.

Doctors are not divine…do your due diligence prior to any major surgery and get second opinions. It may literally save your life.

As I prepare my manuscript for publication submission, I am currently hiding from the COVID-19 virus, for I am told by my doctors that I would not survive it. Part of me wants to just *catch it* and just get it over with, but the fighter in me keeps swinging away. Perhaps I will try my hand at writing and our paths may cross again.

A ꜰᴇᴡ sʜᴏᴜᴛ ᴏᴜᴛs ᴛᴏ Jᴜʟɪᴇ ꜰᴏʀ ʜᴇʀ ᴄᴏɴsᴜʟᴛɪɴɢ,

Aʀʟᴇɴᴇ Bᴀᴋᴇʀ ꜰᴏʀ ᴛʜᴇ ᴄᴏᴠᴇʀ ᴅᴇsɪɢɴ

Aɴᴅ Mᴀʀᴛʏ Sᴡᴀɴ ꜰᴏʀ ʜᴇʀ ᴀʟᴛᴇʀɴᴀᴛɪᴠᴇ ᴛɪᴛʟᴇ "Dᴜᴅᴇ, ᴡʜᴇʀᴇ's ᴍʏ ꜰᴀʟʟᴏᴘɪᴀɴ ᴛᴜʙᴇ?!"